THE FAMILY
FINANCIAL
WORKBOOK

THE FAMILY FINANCIAL WORKBOOK

A Practical Guide to Budgeting

LARRY BURKETT

Moody Press
Chicago

© 1979, 1990, 2000 by
Larry Burkett

Revised Edition, 2000

All Scripture quotations from the (updated) *New American Standard Bible*®, © 1960, 1962, 1963, 1968, 1971, 1972, 1973, 1975, 1977, and 1995 by The Lockman Foundation. Used by permission.

Edited by Adeline Griffith, Crown Financial Ministries.
Some portions of copy contributed by Jeremy White, CPA, PLLC.

ISBN 0-8024-1478-8

5 7 9 10 8 6 4

Printed in the United States of America

FAMILY FINANCIAL WORKBOOK

A Practical Guide to Budgeting

*Make all you can,
save all you can,
give all you can.*

–John Wesley

Contents

Introduction *This Book Is for You*

Chapter

Form 1	Monthly Income and Expenses
Form 2	Variable Expense Planning
Form 3	Budget Percentage Guidelines
Form 4	Budget Analysis
Form 5	Income Allocation
Form 6	Savings Account Allocations
Form 7	Individual Account Page
Form 7a	Checkbook Ledger
Form 8	List of Debts
Form 9	Impulse List

INTRODUCTION
THIS BOOK IS FOR YOU

Congratulations! By purchasing this workbook, you have made a first step toward positive financial changes for you and your family. However, it is only the first step. At Crown Financial Ministries we have observed that some people purchase this workbook with good intentions but never apply the concepts and suggestions.

Improving your finances and your stewardship likely will involve change. Behavioral psychologists say that for change to occur, "The pain to stay the same must be greater than the pain to change." Consider this. If you continue your present financial habits, where will your debts, expenses, and savings be next year? five years from now? at retirement?

This workbook focuses on the most effective tool to understanding and managing the financial resources God gives you. That tool is a budget. Both the grandmother who lived through the Depression and modern-day financial planners agree that you need a budget.

The word *budget* scares many people. Why? They see budgeting as a punishment plan or an impossible task. Unfortunately, this has often been the case with families attempting to correct in one month financial problems that have been developing for several years.

It doesn't have to be that way. A budget is simply a financial plan for the home. This workbook provides a simple, workable plan for home money management. The plan brings finances under God's control and relieves the worry, frustration, and anxiety that come with out-of-control spending. The budget maximizes family finances so that we are more effective for God both spiritually and financially. It is a catalyst for good communication in an area often characterized by conflict.

You may lack financial confidence, perhaps because of prior negative experiences with budgeting. To help you win the battle of your mind, use the following list of truths to overcome the common myths of budgeting.

Budgeting: Myths and Truths

Myth: We have tried a budget once before and it didn't work.

Truth: New skills are not perfected on the first try. Did you ride a bike, cook a gourmet meal, or hit a home run the first time you tried? If you have tried budgeting previously, you are in the best position to succeed, because you can benefit from your previous mistakes and experience. You know it takes effort, and you can be determined to make a lasting change.

Myth: We live on a variable income and, therefore, cannot budget.

Truth: More than anyone, people on variable incomes should budget. Although your income varies, you still need to follow a budget to ensure your expenses do not exceed your average variable income. In Chapter 7, variable income and expenses are discussed further.

Myth: It is impossible to budget for contingencies and unplanned expenses.

Truth: Contingencies are one of the most important items to include in your budget. Although you may not know exactly what will happen, you know there may be some doctor visits and car repairs. The sooner you begin your budget and establish some history of experience, the better you can predict future occurrences. Companies estimate contingencies. In fact, an entire industry (insurance) is built around estimating contingencies. You can build contingencies into your budget.

Myth: We are not mathematically inclined.

Truth: A budget does not involve calculus, geometry, or complex algebraic equations. Knowing addition and subtraction is enough. Other tools exist, such as the calculator or computer, to eliminate any math that may be difficult or tedious.

Myth: We are not the "financial" types.

Truth: Although the budget is the most basic and important financial tool, you do not need a business degree, stock market knowledge, or an accounting background to establish a budget. You are simply keeping track of the money coming in and going out.

Myth: We don't earn enough income to budget.

Truth: You definitely need a budget. The smaller your income, the stronger your need for a budget. When you budget, you limit excess spending, and it's as if your income grows.

Myth: We earn too much income to worry about a budget.

Truth: Although you may be blessed with an above-average income, a budget can help you be a good steward with your surplus. Unfortunately, as incomes rise the expenses rise at the same or greater rate. Setting a plan and keeping a budget will help you use your growing income for the benefit of your family and others.

Myth: We have money problems because we don't have enough income.

Truth: Usually, financial problems result from overspending. Budgeting can help you locate the areas in which spending may be out of control.

Myth: We don't have time to keep track of a budget.

Truth: It takes far more time to handle a financial mess than it does to keep your finances in order. Remember that adage: An ounce of prevention is worth a pound of cure. Keeping a budget takes less time than you think. After you establish your budget, it takes only thirty minutes to an hour per week to maintain.[1]

Thousands of families have successfully used this workbook as a tool to help them manage their finances practically and biblically. This workbook is designed for you to use, not just read. It includes the following design features and graphics.

Budget Forms—Throughout this workbook, we illustrate examples of various completed forms. Chapter 10 includes blank budget and planning forms to prepare your own budget. You may photocopy these for personal use.

Bible Verses—Beyond the practical suggestions, you will find Scripture references giving the biblical principles.

Motivational Reminders—Special sections for you to copy and place in a strategic spot (i.e., bathroom mirror, refrigerator door, or car dashboard). Use these to motivate yourself to stay with the course and improve your finances.

[1]Jeremy L. White, CPA, PLLC

The love of money as a possession—as distinguished from the love of money as a means to the enjoyments and realities of life—will be recognized for what it is, a somewhat disgusting morbidity.

–John Maynard Keynes

Introduction
This Book
Is for You

Living Proof Testimonies—Much shame is often associated with the area of finances. It is easy to feel like you are alone and no one else has been where you are. To encourage you, we include at the end of each chapter unedited testimonies sent to Crown Financial Ministries from people just like you. These are people who have applied the principles in this workbook and now say, "Been there, done that, thank you, and to God be the glory." The first examples are below.

Living Proof Testimonies

A married couple has been on a budget for more than two years and is now debt-free.

"What a blessing that has been! For years and years we spent money simply because we had it in our checking account without any planning for future expenses. Being on a budget has brought such freedom to our lives. (I can't believe how foolishly we spent money in the past.)"

*   *   *

A couple owed a significant amount of debt and they both lost their jobs. They used credit cards for groceries and gas. They started on a budget and are out of debt, except for college loans.

"It wasn't until after we were in desperate financial difficulty that we learned what a budget is all about and how to use one. We're on our way to debt freedom. May God richly bless your ministry as you help Christians learn God's truth about finances."

IF YOU READ NOTHING ELSE... READ THIS!

O money, money, money, I'm not necessarily one of those who thinks thee holy, but I often stop to wonder how thou canst go out so fast when thou comest in so slowly.
—Ogden Nash

IF YOU READ NOTHING ELSE... READ THIS!

CHAPTER 1

Because the urgent often crowds out the important, sometimes we don't have time to read and absorb the very information we need. If you like headlines and bullet points, then this quick summary is for you. It is not an exact outline of this workbook, but it provides a quick reference of key points. After finishing the workbook, continue to use this chapter as a reminder.

1. Principles dealing with home finances

    a. Set your goals—with your family.

    b. Use a written budget.

    c. Provide for the Lord's work first.

    d. Limit credit.

    e. Think before buying.

    f. Practice saving money regularly.

    g. Get out of debt.

    h. Avoid speculative investments.

    i. Avoid indulgences and lavishness.

    j. Seek good Christian counsel.

    k. Stick to your plans.

2. Purpose of a budget

    a. To define income versus expenses.

    b. To detect problem areas.

    c. To provide a written plan for spending and saving.

    d. To aid in communication and accountability.

    e. To schedule money in and out of the home.

3. What a budget will do

    a. Help you visualize your goals.

    b. Provide a written point of reference for husband and wife.

    c. Help family communications.

    d. Provide a written reminder.

    e. Reflect your spending habits.

4. What a budget will not do

    a. Solve all your immediate problems.

    b. Make you use it.

    c. Eliminate all decision making.

    d. Balance by itself.

5. Getting started with your budget

    a. Understand your current financial position.

       • Use a thirty-day expense diary or notebook.

       • Use a checking account ledger.

       • List all debts with amount due, monthly payment, due date, and interest rate.

    b. Creating a family budget

       • Calculate income.

       • Calculate fixed expenses.

       • Calculate variable expenses.

       • Design your budget with categories.

       • Pray for wisdom: in setting your budget goals, for self-control in spending, and for discipline in maintaining plans.

    c. Using a budget

       • Keep it visible and available for use.

       • Set achievable goals and estimates.

       • Keep records up to date.

       • Establish a set time and day to review it with your spouse.

       • Make changes as circumstances and plans warrant.

Motivational Reminders

"Think before you buy." Consider these questions before a purchase, particularly a more expensive or unplanned one.

- Is it necessary?
- Does it reflect your Christian ethic?
- Is it the best buy?
- Is it an impulse item?
- Would my spouse agree with the decision to purchase?
- Does it add to or detract from the family?
- Is it a highly depreciable item?
- Does it require costly upkeep?

God can have our money and not have our hearts, but he cannot have our hearts without having our money.

–R. Kent Hughes

Living Proof Testimony

This couple owed $30,000 in debt as a result of poor financial decisions.

"We were not tithing and could hardly afford to feed ourselves. We did not want to file bankruptcy. We had created the mess and wanted to do the right thing and pay off all our creditors. We began tithing on our gross. We could not afford your budgeting guide so I went to the local Christian bookstore and studied the workbook. Larry, it worked. That was over three years ago and we have been debt free for eight months now."

FAIL TO PLAN, PLAN TO FAIL

We'll hold the distinction of being the only nation in the history of the world that ever went to the poor house in an automobile.
— Will Rogers

FAIL TO PLAN, PLAN TO FAIL

Planning is an essential element in any financial program, but particularly for Christians. God is an orderly provider and expects the same from us.

Why Should We Plan?

1. God wants us to be knowledgeable about the assets He has entrusted to us. *"Know well the condition of your flocks, and pay attention to your herds"* (Proverbs 27:23). For herds or flocks, substitute what you actually have.

2. We are to be an active part of God's plan as we exercise our minds and abilities. *"Commit your works to the Lord and your plans will be established"* (Proverbs 16:3). We are required to plan and to commit those plans to the Lord.

3. Plan with the future in mind. *"Which one of you, when he wants to build a tower, does not first sit down and calculate the cost to see if he has enough to complete it?"* (Luke 14:28). That means we should anticipate the unforeseen.

4. Each Christian should know God's provision for him individually and be content with it. *"Godliness actually is a means of great gain when accompanied by contentment"* (1 Timothy 6:6). When godliness and contentment work together in our hearts and minds, they bring gain–both financially and, more importantly, spiritually.

Considering Your Family Plan

Family planning is more than considering the number of children to have. Every Christian should establish a long-range family plan. What do you want for your family? Have you ever brought your family together to pray about how God wants you to live?

Fail to Plan, Plan to Fail

Your budget doesn't determine your family plan. Your family plan determines your budget. Your budget is a reflection of your family goals and direction.

Key elements of your family plan include the following.

1. *Decide a career path.* Too often we choose a job based only on its pay. There are other issues to consider. What kind of career or job best allows you to meet your church and family commitments? Will both the husband and the wife work? Are you willing to move with your job, or are you committed to a geographical area more than to a job? (Note: Crown Financial Ministries offers a comprehensive vocational assessment. Visit our Web site at www.crown.org.)

2. *Plan for children and other dependents.* Beyond the number of children, do you plan for one parent to stay at home? Will the children attend public school, private school, or remain at home for school? Is it likely you will have to provide for another family member, such as an elderly parent?

3. *Have a family giving plan.* Why should God trust you with a surplus? Do you have financial goals specifically related to giving to His kingdom? Does your family manage excess money well? Do your children understand a proper attitude about material possessions? Pray together as a family about ministries and humanitarian needs around the world. Pray to increase your giving as God gives to you.

4. *Have a surplus plan.* You should establish a plan in the event that you accumulate wealth faster than anticipated. Scripture is clear on this point: God's surplus is to be shared. This is God's plan for Christians, but unless you have a predetermined plan for increase, expenses are often adjusted to offset any increases. Consequently, there will never be a surplus to share.

5. *Have an estate plan.* Do you have a plan for how much to leave your family after your death? God's plan is to provide for the needs of our family members and, if possible, provide for certain financial goals in our family plan (such as college education) in the event of an untimely death.

Setting Your Family Plan

Communication is vital to family financial planning. To enhance that communication, some questions are listed for both husband and wife. I suggest that each of you do them separately. Write every answer as if your spouse were asking the question. Then, during a time when you won't be interrupted, evaluate these together. Begin your evaluation by praying about your time together and opening your hearts to the Holy Spirit.

The questions are intended to enrich the discussions of mature, communicating Christian couples. They are not intended to become an additional source of friction for couples who are already void of communication and defensive about finances. Use them as tools of love, not ammunition for war.

CHAPTER

Having money to burn is a good way to start a fire you can't put out.

—Anon

Family Goals

1. What are our family goals? _____
   _____
   _____

2. Are we achieving our family goals? If not, how could we better communicate, plan, and achieve these goals? _____
   _____
   _____

3. a. (Wife asks) What can I do to help you fulfill your responsibilities as spiritual leader of our family? _____
   _____
   _____

   b. (Husband asks) How can I better fulfill my responsibilities as spiritual leader?
   _____
   _____

4. Do you feel we are meeting the spiritual needs of our family? _____

_____

_____

5. What kinds of family devotions should we have? _____

_____

_____

6. List the responsibilities stated for the husband and wife in the following passages:

1 Peter 3:1-2 _____

Colossians 3:18-19 _____

1 Timothy 2:11-15 _____

1 Corinthians 11:3 _____

Ephesians 5:17-33 _____

7. Do you think we have a consistent prayer life together? _____

_____

8. Do you believe we are adequately involved in our local church? _____

_____

9. Do you feel we are meeting the physical needs of our family? _____

_____

10. Should we improve our eating habits? _____

_____

11. Should we get more exercise? _____

_____

12. Do we make good use of our time? For example, do we watch too much TV? Should we have more hobbies? read more? _____

_____

13. How and when should we discipline our children? What do you think is the biblical viewpoint of discipline? _____

_____

_____

14. List the responsibilities of parents and their children in the following passages.

Colossians 3:18-19 _____

Hebrews 12:5-11 _____

Proverbs 3:11-12 _____

Ephesians 6:4 _____

15. What kind of instruction and training should be given to children in the home?

_____

_____

Financial Goals

1. Do you think I handle money properly? _____

_____

CHAPTER

Put not your trust in money, but put your money in trust.

—Oliver Wendell Holmes

2. How could I better manage our money?_____

_____

3. Do you think I am

too frugal? _____

too extravagant? _____

about right? _____

Why? _____

_____

_____

4. Do you think I accept financial responsibilities well?_____

_____

5. Do you think we communicate financial goals well?_____

_____

6. What is your immediate financial goal? _____

_____

7. What is your primary goal for this year?_____

_____

8. What is your plan for our children's education? _____

_____

9. What is your retirement goal?_____

_____

10. What do you think about tithing?

Is tithing necessary? _____

How much? _____

Where should it go? _____

11. How do you feel about giving in general? Would you like to give more?

_____

_____

12. Do you like the way we live? _____

_____

13. What changes do you think we should make? _____

_____

Living Proof Testimonies

A couple has used this budget workbook and forms for about three years.

"It is amazing what God has done in us spiritually as well as in our marriage. It has definitely lowered the stress in our relationship and we continue to work on being better stewards of the money God has given us. We are free in so many ways."

* * *

A woman wrote, saying that she and her husband decided before marriage that they would live on his income and save hers. They are debt free and buying a house that can be paid off with the husband's salary.

"The financial freedom we have is wonderful and will allow me the option of staying home when we have our children. We thank God for allowing us this financial freedom and thank God for ministries like yours that give hope and encouragement to God's people."

CHAPTER 3

EVERYBODY NEEDS A BUDGET!

The way to stop financial joy-riding is to arrest the chauffeur, not the automobile. —*Woodrow Wilson*

EVERYBODY NEEDS A BUDGET!

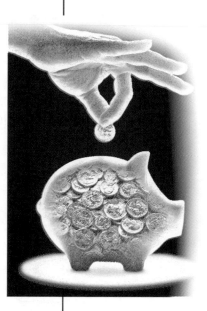

Financial bondage can result from a lack of money and overspending. It also can be caused from the misuse of an abundance of money. Some families have enough money to be undisciplined and get away with it (financially speaking). True financial freedom requires us to be good stewards and make the most of every dollar.

An essential part of obtaining financial freedom is living within your means, or spending no more than you make on a monthly basis. This was the normal way of living and thinking only a generation or two ago. Today, however, society, advertisers, retailers, and peers pressure you to live beyond your means and to use borrowed money to provide normal living expenses. If you have a significant salary and expect it to increase, it is hard to say no to easy credit.

But if you consistently spend more than you earn, then you are making your present financial situation difficult and your future miserable. After you consistently spend less than you earn, you begin to make significant strides toward financial freedom.

A budget is the best tool to help you spend less than you earn. It is rare to find a person in financial difficulty that maintains a budget. A budget is simply an income and spending plan. It is simple in theory but challenging in practice. Remember that a budget doesn't constrain you; it helps you maximize spending in each area.

The Three Levels of Spending

You must have the self-discipline to control spending and keep needs, wants, and desires in their proper relationship. Needs, wants, and desires can be incorporated into your budget.

Needs

"If we have food and covering, with these we shall be content" (1 Timothy 6:8).

Needs are the purchases necessary to provide your basic requirements, such as food, clothing, lodging, medical coverage. In our culture we easily mistake wants for needs: "I need that." We must learn how to discern true needs and admit wants. We also must take responsibility for purchasing needs wisely. If your child has outgrown his or her shoes, you have a wide choice of styles, colors, and prices from which to choose. Find something that fits your budget.

Needs comprise the greatest portion of your budget. Commit your needs to the Lord, be obedient to His Word, follow His principles, and watch Him provide for your family.

Wants

"Your adornment must not be merely external–braiding the hair, and wearing gold jewelry, or putting on dresses; but let it be the hidden person of the heart, with the imperishable quality of a gentle and quiet spirit, which is precious in the sight of God" (1 Peter 3:3-4).

It is not wrong to have material wants; rather, it is quite natural. The trouble comes from wanting too much, wanting too soon, and being unhappy if we can't have all we want. Admitting wants is an important step toward creating a balanced, workable budget. Wants often involve choices about the quality of goods to be used, such as steak versus hamburger. If your budget allows, schedule for wants that would bless your family; but, remember that external beauty and luxuries are not what bring lasting happiness!

Desires

"Do not love the world nor the things in the world. If anyone loves the world, the love of the Father is not in him. For all that is in the world, the lust of the flesh and the lust of the eyes and the boastful pride of life, is not from the Father, but is from the world" (1 John 2:15-16).

According to God's plan, these are choices that can be made only out of surplus funds, after all other obligations have been met. Long-term goals and dreams should be committed to prayer and scheduled into the budget as possible.

Everybody Needs a Budget!

See the following examples to clarify the differences between needs, wants, and desires.

Category	Needs	Wants	Desires
Clothing	New clothes from discount store or used clothing store	New clothes from department store	Designer clothes, custom tailored
Food	Tuna	Shrimp	Lobster
Transportation	Used family car or public transportation	New family car or used luxury vehicle	New luxury vehicle

If you have money, it doth not stay, but this way and that it wastes amain.

–Francios Villon

God cares about the house you live in, the car you drive, where you work, whether your wife should work, where your children attend college, and even the food you eat. Have you ever prayed about those things? If you haven't, how can you expect to know what God's will is for your family?

Establish priorities with your family, particularly your children. When your children approach you with a request, help them understand the difference between needs, wants, and desires.

If it is a need, it should be supplied; however, if it is a want or a desire, perhaps your child should earn it or request it for a birthday. When children learn that they must earn some of their wants and desires, they make quick adjustments. Comic books are weighed against the value of a new baseball bat, a cheap plastic toy against a new bicycle.

Be consistent and fair but firm. Just as God will not grant you whims that work to your detriment, you must hold the same position with your children. As is true with teaching anything, you as the teacher will learn more about needs, wants, and desires for your own life than the student–your child.

The Big Picture: The Divisions of Income

Before we discuss the details of budgeting, you must first recognize the divisions of income.

- The *first* part belongs to God. It is returned to Him as a tithe in recognition that He owns all we have. We are merely stewards (managers).

> *"Will a man rob God? Yet you are robbing Me! But you say, 'How have we robbed You?' In tithes and offerings"* (Malachi 3:8).

- Then, of course, the government wants its share, in the form of taxes.

> *"He said to them, 'Then render to Caesar the things that are Caesar's; and to God the things that are God's'"* (Matthew 22:21).

- The portion available after tithe and taxes is termed **Net Spendable Income.**

Gross Income minus Tithe and Taxes equals **Net Spendable Income.**

From the Net Spendable Income, you meet your family needs, such as Housing, Food, Medical, and so on.

> *"But if anyone does not provide for his own, and especially for those of his household, he has denied the faith and is worse than an unbeliever"* (1 Timothy 5:8).

- Then, you must fulfill your commitments from past overspending. God says to pay your debts.

> *"The wicked borrows and does not pay back"* (Psalms 37:21).

- Faithful management will yield a fifth portion: a surplus. The creation of a surplus should be a major goal for the Christian. This is the surplus that allows us to respond to the needs of others.

> *"At this present time your abundance being a supply for their need, so that their abundance also may become a supply for your need, that there may be equality"* (2 Corinthians 8:14).

Even if a family is not in debt, to maximize the surplus, their finances should be budget controlled. In addition to responding to the needs of others, it's the surplus that provides the flexibility to meet emergencies without credit. That surplus can also be used to invest and multiply your assets.

Everybody Needs a Budget!

Motivational Reminders

Why is it hard to have financial self-control? Here are the obstacles to good planning and budgeting.

- Social pressures to own more "things."
- The attitude that "more is better" regardless of the cost.
- The use of credit to delay necessary decisions.
- No surplus available to cope with rising prices and unexpected expenses.
- Offsetting increases in income by increasing the level of spending.

Often all it takes to start down the road to bankruptcy is a small raise in pay.

—Anon

Living Proof Testimonies

A woman lived paycheck to paycheck, paying all year for last year's Christmas gifts she bought on credit cards. Eight years ago she accepted the Lord. She wrote,

"I started on a budget, lived by God's biblical principles, and we are now debt free. Totally. I haven't carried a balance on a credit card for years. PRAISE GOD!"

*　　*　　*

Sixteen years ago, a young bride came across the *Financial Planning Workbook* (the original title of this workbook) in a secondhand bookstore. She and her husband live by the biblical financial principles found in this book. They live in a home on five acres that is paid for and drive older vehicles with no debt. She has stayed home to raise her children.

"Much of this wouldn't have been true if God hadn't placed your workbook into my hands those many years ago. Neither my husband nor I had been taught how to manage money; our children are much wiser. Thank you for your willingness to speak frankly regarding Christians and their finances."

WHERE ARE YOU NOW?

A man's treatment of money is the most decisive test of his character—how he makes it and how he spends it.
—Moffat

WHERE ARE YOU NOW?

CHAPTER 4

Tracking Leads to Budgeting

Starting a budget is just like starting on a trip. You cannot set a course without first determining where you are.

Most people that come for financial counseling have little idea of how much they spend each month or where it goes. They only know that there is "more month than money."

Before you set your budget, you need to see where you are by making a list of whom you owe, how much you spend every month, and what you are spending your money on. Crown's financial counselors complete these same steps with each counselee. During the first counseling session, the counselors list the debts of the counselees and assign homework to them to track their spending.

It works in counseling sessions and it will work for you. How can you stop the bleeding if you don't know where the bleeding is? Here is what you need to do.

List all your debts and total them. Although this is a simple step, many have never made a list of all they owe. It can be discouraging, but it can also be the lightning rod to action. From Chapter 10, use Form 8, List of Debts, to record your basic debt information. Here is an example.

To Whom Owed	Phone Number	Payoff	Payments Left	Monthly Payment	Due Date	Interest Rate
VISA	800-999-9999	$ 1,679	38	$ 75	20th	18
Dept. Store	800-000-0000	$ 5,342	85	$ 150	28th	24
Car Loan	123-123-1234	$ 18,679	52	$ 430	15th	11
Mortgage Co.	777-777-7777	$ 99,000	346	$ 735	1st	8
Total		$124,700		$1,390		

Be sure to include all debts. Watch out for hidden debts. A common error later in budgeting is to overlook non-monthly debts such as family loans, doctor bills, or bank notes. Thus, when payments come due there's no budget allocation for them.

Write down every expense. Both the husband and wife should list cash expenditures, checks, and credit card charges. If either spends $1.50 at the vending machine at work, write it down. If you go out to eat and charge the meal, write it down.

Organize each expense into meaningful categories. You do not want to simply repeat your checkbook register or have a fifteen-page list of expenses. To analyze your spending, it is helpful to know how much you spent on each category; for example, groceries, insurance, or entertainment. Start with the following categories (this will help you get familiar with the categories you will use later for budgeting).

- Income
- Tithe
- Taxes
- Housing
- Food
- Automobile
- Insurance
- Debts
- Entertainment/Recreation
- Clothing
- Savings
- Medical
- Miscellaneous
- Investments
- School/Child Care

The method of recording is not as important as that you do it! You may use a spiral notebook with one page for each category, a spreadsheet computer program with a row of categories at the top, or a personal finance software program. (CFC has a software budget program called *Money Matters 2000*. Visit the Web site at www.crown.org.)

Total each category at the end of a month and review the totals. It is very important for both the husband and wife to be involved in this review. Review your results in a non-pressured, relaxed atmosphere. After the children are in bed, turn off the television, pop some popcorn, and pray that God will help you discern your current situation. Remember that accusing each other will not solve problems.[1]

[1]Jeremy L. White, CPA, PLLC

Tracking your expenses may expose some unpleasant trends. That's okay. Becoming aware of these unpleasant trends then leads to planning your spending, limiting some categories, and saving for others. At that moment, you have begun budgeting!

For example, let's say that Dave and Nicole Smith read this chapter and decide to get started listing their debts and tracking their expenses. During their review session at the end of their first month, Dave looks at the totals and asks, "How did we spend $350 for Entertainment/Recreation in only one month?"

"Let's look at the detail here in our notebook," Nicole says as she scans the page that lists their Entertainment expenses. "It looks like most of the $350 was for eating out at restaurants. That seems like a lot."

Dave nods in agreement. "Especially when I see that we have three credit card debts that we are making only the minimum payments on. Why don't we try to cut down on going out to eat and use that money to make larger payments on our credit card debt?"

With that last statement, the Smiths are moving toward budgeting. They have not set a formal budget yet. But by listing their debts, tracking their spending, and reviewing their current situation, they have started planning and are ready to start budgeting.

CHAPTER

It is thrifty to prepare today for the wants of tomorrow.

–Aesop ("The Ant and the Grasshopper")

Motivational Reminders

Your list of debts can serve as a "payoff goal" sheet. Begin with a goal of eliminating the smallest debt first, then double up on the next debt until it is paid, and so on until all debts are eliminated.

Write here your three lowest debts. Your mission is to focus, pay down, and eliminate. Post this list where you can see it often as motivation. Take satisfaction in crossing off each debt when it is paid.

To Whom Owed	Phone Number	Payoff Amount	Payments Left	Monthly Payment	Due Date	Interest Rate

Where Are You Now?

A woman was given the *Financial Planning Workbook* (the original title of this book) by her mother seven years ago when she and her husband owed $30,000 in consumer debt and back taxes.

"We started paying off our debt and now owe only $600 on credit cards that will be paid off in two months. We plan to have our cars paid off next summer and are inspired to be debt free."

SETTING YOUR BUDGET

Money doesn't change men, it unmasks them. If a man is naturally selfish or arrogant or greedy, the money brings that out, is all.
— Henry Ford, automaker

SETTING YOUR BUDGET

CHAPTER 5

After you have listed your debts and tracked your expenses for at least one or two months, you will have an initial view of your current spending level. But remember that tracking your spending only shows where you are, not where you want to go.

Setting your budget shows where you want to go. How do you know where to set spending limits and income plans? What should your level of spending be for specific categories?

You can find the answers to these questions about budget amounts in the following three areas.

1. **Your family goals and vision.** If you are planning to have four kids with the mother at home and live in a small town, then your budget will look different than a childless couple who hope to go to seminary in a big city. The purpose of the planning discussion in Chapter 4 is so your family vision and desires will give direction to your budget.

2. **Your present financial commitments.** If you have a very large debt burden, then you have already set much of your present budget with past overspending. You will likely have little available income to decide how to spend.

3. **Your spending habits compared to others at a similar income level, also called a guideline budget.** Although the first two answers above are internal benchmarks for setting a budget, using a guideline budget is an external measure to help set your budget. The rest of this chapter will focus on comparing your spending level to a guideline budget.

What Is a Guideline Budget?

A guideline budget is family spending divided into percentages to help determine the *proper balance* in each category of the budget–for example, Housing, Food, and Automobile.

The primary use of the guideline is to *indicate problem areas*; it is *not* an absolute. The percentages illustrated in Figure 5.1 are based on a family of four people with incomes ranging from $25,000 to $115,000 per year. Above or below those limits, the percentages may change, according to family situations and needs. In the lower income levels, basic family needs will dominate the income distribution.

Purpose of a Guideline Budget

The Guideline Budget is developed to determine a standard against which to compare present spending patterns. It serves as a basis for determining areas of overspending that are creating the greatest problems. Additionally, it helps to determine where adjustments need to be made. If you are overspending, the percentage guideline can be used as a goal for budgeting. Although the percentages are only guides and are not absolutes, they do help to establish upper levels of spending.

For example, a family spending 40 percent or more of their Net Spendable Income on Housing will have difficulty balancing their budget. There is little flexibility in most family incomes to absorb excessive spending on Housing or Auto.

Guideline Percentages

The *Net Spendable Income* is used to calculate the ideal spending for each budget category. (Remember, Net Spendable Income is your gross income less your tithe and taxes.) If taxes are known, then actual amounts can be used. In the example shown in Figure 5.2, Net Spendable Income is $1,769 per month. For the Housing category, 38 percent of equals $672 per month. Therefore, as a guideline, the Housing expense should be less than $672 per month for payments, taxes, utilities, and upkeep.

Note that in some detailed subcategories absolutes are impossible with variables like utilities and taxes. For the overall categories, you must adjust percentages within ranges under Housing, Food, and Auto. Those three together cannot exceed 66 percent. For example, if 40 percent is used for Housing, the percentage for Food and Auto must be reduced.

PERCENTAGE GUIDE FOR FAMILY INCOME
Family of Four
(The Net Spendable percentages are applicable to Head of Household family of three, as well)

Gross Household Income	$25,000 or less	$35,000	$45,000	$55,000	$65,000	$85,000	$115,000
1. Tithe	10%	10%	10%	10%	10%	10%	10%
2. Tax	5.1%	14.9%	17.9%	19.9%	21.8%	25.8%	28.1%
Net Spendable Income (per month)	$21,225	$26,285	$32,445	$38,555	$44,330	$54,570	$71,185
Net Spendable percentages below add to 100%.							
3. Housing	38%	36%	32%	30%	30%	30%	29%
4. Food	14%	12%	13%	12%	11%	11%	11%
5. Auto	14%	12%	13%	14%	14%	13%	13%
6. Insurance	5%	5%	5%	5%	5%	5%	5%
7. Debts	5%	5%	5%	5%	5%	5%	5%
8. Enter./Recreation	4%	6%	6%	7%	7%	7%	8%
9. Clothing	5%	5%	5%	6%	6%	7%	7%
10. Savings	5%	5%	5%	5%	5%	5%	5%
11. Medical	5%	4%	4%	4%	4%	4%	4%
12. Miscellaneous	5%	5%	5%	5%	5%	5%	5%
13. Investments[1]	—	5%	7%	7%	8%	8%	8%
If you have this expense below, the percentage shown must be deducted from other budget categories.							
14. School/Child Care[2]	8%	6%	5%	5%	5%	5%	5%
15. Unallocated Surplus Income[3]	—	—	—	—	—	—	—

1. This category is used for long-term investment planning, such as caring for elderly parents or retirement.
2. This category is added as a guide only. If you have this expense, the percentage shown must be deducted from other budget categories.
3. This category is used when surplus income is received.

Figure 5.1

BUDGET PERCENTAGE GUIDELINES

Salary for guideline = $_____25,000_____/year[1]

Gross Income Per Month $_____2,083_____

1. Tithe   (_10_ % of Gross) (_____2,083_____) = $ _____208_____

2. Tax   (_5.1_% of Gross) (_____2,083_____) = $ _____106_____

Net Spendable Income $_____1,769_____

3. Housing   (_38_ % of Net) (_____1,769_____) = $ _____672_____

4. Food   (_14_ % of Net) (_____1,769_____) = $ _____248_____

5. Auto   (_14_ % of Net) (_____1,769_____) = $ _____248_____

6. Insurance   (_5_ % of Net) (_____1,769_____) = $ _____88_____

7. Debts   (_5_ % of Net) (_____1,769_____) = $ _____88_____

8. Entertainment/ Recreation   (_4_ % of Net) (_____1,769_____) = $ _____71_____

9. Clothing   (_5_ % of Net) (_____1,769_____) = $ _____88_____

10. Savings   (_5_ % of Net) (_____1,769_____) = $ _____88_____

11. Medical   (_5_ % of Net) (_____1,769_____) = $ _____88_____

12. Miscellaneous (_5_ % of Net) (_____1,769_____) = $ _____88_____

13. Investments   (_0_ % of Net)[1] (_____) = $ _____

14. School/ Child Care   (_8_ % of Net)[2] (_____) = $ _____

Total (Cannot exceed Net Spendable Income) $ _____1,767_____[3]

15. Unallocated Surplus Income[4]   (_____N/A_____) = $ _____

1. Considering the given obligations at this income level, there is no surplus for investing long term.
2. For this example, this percentage has *not* been factored into the total percentages shown for net income.
3. Because of rounding to the nearest dollar, this figure may not match the Net Spendable Income exactly. You may add or deduct the difference from any category total to make an exact match.
4. This category is not part of the budget system but can be used to record and show disbursements of unallocated surplus income. This also provides a good record of income for tax purposes.

Figure 5.2

Budget Analysis

After determining the present spending level (where you are), and reviewing the guideline percentages (where you should be), the task becomes one of developing a new budget that handles the areas of overspending. Keep in mind that the total expenditures must not exceed the Net Spendable Income. If you have more spendable income than expenses, you will need to control spending to maximize your surplus.

The Budget Analysis (Form 4) provides space for summarizing both existing expenses and guideline expenses on one sheet. The total amounts of each category from the Monthly Income and Expenses sheet (Form 1) and from the Budget Percentage Guidelines (Form 3) should be transferred to the appropriate columns on the Budget Analysis page. See Figure 5.3 below. The forms are in Chapter 10.

CHAPTER 5

Nobody ever went broke saving money.

–Anon

BUDGET ANALYSIS

Per Year $ 25,000
Per Month $ 2,083

Net Spendable Income
Per Month $ 1,769

MONTHLY PAYMENT CATEGORY	EXISTING BUDGET	MONTHLY GUIDELINE BUDGET	DIFFERENCE + OR -	NEW MONTHLY BUDGET
1. Tithe	125	208	+ 83	208
2. Tax	500	106	- 394	106
Net Spendable Income (per month)	$ 1,458	$ 1,769	$ + 311	$ 1,769
3. Housing	554	672	+ 118	672
4. Food	230	248	+ 18	248
5. Auto	285	248	- 37	248
6. Insurance	39	88	+ 49	39
7. Debts	90	88	- 2	90
8. Enter./Recreation	100	71	- 29	90
9. Clothing	50	88	+ 38	88
10. Savings	0	88	+ 88	88
11. Medical	20	88	+ 68	88
12. Miscellaneous	145	88	- 57	116
13. Investments	0	N/A	0	0
14. School/Child Care[1]	0	142	+ 142	0
Totals (Items 3-14)	$ 1,513	$ 1,767[2]		$ 1,767[2]
15. Unallocated Surplus Income[3]	0	N/A	0	+ 61

1. This category not included in totals for this example.
2. Because of rounding to the nearest dollar, this figure may not match the Net Spendable Income exactly. You may add or deduct the difference from any category total to make an exact match.
3. This amount was derived from a garage sale. It is not part of your monthly budget.

Step One: Compare

Compare the Existing Budget and Monthly Guideline columns for the various categories. Note the difference, plus or minus, in the Difference column. A negative notation indicates a deficit; a positive notation indicates a surplus. The budget shown is the actual spending of a typical family of four.

Step Two: Analyze

After comparing the *Existing Budget and Monthly Guideline* columns, decisions must be made about overspending. It may be possible to reduce some areas to compensate for overspending in others. For example, if Housing expenditures are more than 38 percent, it may be necessary to sacrifice in areas like Entertainment/Recreation, Miscellaneous, and Auto. If debts exceed 5 percent, then the problems are compounded. Ultimately, the decision becomes one of where and how to cut back.

It is not necessary for your new budget to fit the guideline budget. It is necessary that your new budget does not exceed your Net Spendable Income.

It is usually at this point that husband-wife communication is so important. No one person can make a budget work, because it may involve a family financial sacrifice. Without a willingness on the part of both spouses to sacrifice and establish discipline, no budget will succeed.

Note the flexibility gained if the family is not in debt. That 5 percent is available for use somewhere else in the budget.

Step Three: Decide

Once the total picture is reviewed, it is necessary to decide where adjustments must be made and the spending reduced. It may be necessary to consider a change in housing, automobiles, insurance, private schools, or other areas.

The *minimum* objective of any budget should be to meet your family's needs without creating any further debt.

If there are debt problems, then begin by destroying all credit cards and other sources of credit. It may be necessary to negotiate with creditors to pay smaller amounts per month. It's better to establish an amount you can pay than to promise an amount you can't pay. (Note: For someone to assist in negotiating with your creditors, contact the Consumer Credit Counseling Service at 1-888-771-HOPE.)

Beware of consolidation loans, refinancing, and more borrowing. They are not the solutions; they are merely treatments of the symptoms. The solution comes from discipline, sacrifice, and trusting God to supply all needs.

Following are how the adjustments were made on our example.

Tithe: The tithe was increased to 10 percent of gross income.

Taxes: Taxes were reduced by increasing the Form W-4 allowances by one. When all deductions were considered, this family was withholding too much in tax with respect to gross income.

Housing: Housing was increased to $672.

Food: Note 16 percent of Net Spendable Income was being spent. A target amount of $248 was set. Perhaps this can be improved on with wise shopping.

Auto: Nearly 20 percent of Net Spendable Income was being spent. Transportation will be adjusted to $248 per month by reducing the insurance coverage.

Insurance: This figure was increased to $88. This might be a good time to closely evaluate your insurance needs for now and in the future.

Debts: More than 6 percent was allocated to existing debts. Credit cards were canceled. This shows commitment and paves the way for paying off these debts totally in future months.

Entertainment/Recreation: This category was reduced to $71 per month, at least until debts are paid. Caution: Don't cut this out; cut it back.

Clothing: This allocation was increased from $50 to $88 per month.

Savings: This was increased to $88. Get in the habit of saving. It's your best protection against future debt.

Medical: This was another under-allocated category. It was increased to $88 per month.

Miscellaneous: This category was reduced to $88 per month. If the new budgeted amount is not enough, then another category, such as Entertainment/Recreation or Clothing, will have to be reduced.

Investments: Once an adequate emergency fund is established, additional income may be invested for long-term goals.

School/Child Care: The amount allowed is $142. When money is needed for this category, other categories must be adjusted.

Unallocated Surplus Income: The $61 surplus income this month resulted from a garage sale; and it will be placed in this category for future use as needed or directed to debt reduction or investments.

CHAPTER 5

The money you intend to save draws no interest.

–Anon

After determining your new budget by referring to guidelines and current spending, you are ready to begin making your budget work.

Living Proof Testimonies

These two married couples are on budgets and enjoying the benefits.

One couple has been on a budget for more than two years, is debt-free, and writes,

"What a blessing that [budget] *has been! For years and years we spent money simply because we had it in our checking account without any planning for future expenses. Being on a budget has brought such freedom to our lives. (I can't believe how foolishly we spent money in the past.)"*

*   *   *

Another couple who have used the Crown budget workbook and forms for about three years wrote,

"It is amazing what God has done in us spiritually as well as in our marriage. It [living within their means on a budget] *has definitely lowered the stress in our relationship and we continue to work on being better stewards of the money God has given us. We are free in so many ways."*

Setting
Your
Budget

MAKING YOUR BUDGET WORK

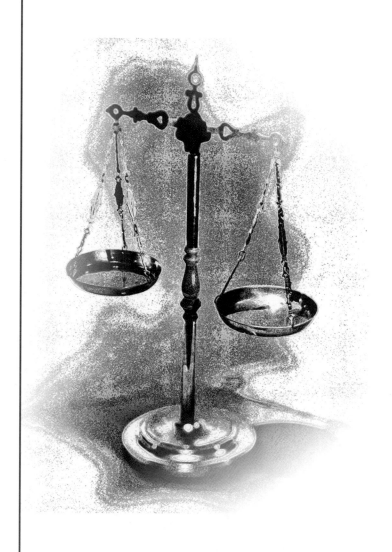

All our material riches will avail us little if we do not use them to expand the opportunities of our people.
—John F. Kennedy

MAKING YOUR BUDGET WORK

Choosing a Budget Method

A budget that is not used is a waste of time and effort. The most common reason people discard a budget is because it is too complicated. The method of budgeting is not so important. Remember, the important aim is to plan a level of spending for each category and know how close you are to that level.

The following are possible budget methods.

Personal finance software—Software eliminates some of the tedious tasks of bookkeeping, improves accuracy, and prints reports quickly and easily. Crown has developed its *Money Matters* software to include the principles and methods included in this workbook. (See Chapter 9, "Financial Resources and Tools" for more information or call 1-800-722-1976.)

Cash envelope system—In the past, many employers paid wages in cash. To control spending, families established an effective "cash envelope" system. After dividing their available money into the various budget categories (Housing, Food, Clothing), families kept the cash in individual envelopes.

As a need or payment came due, money was withdrawn from the proper envelope and spent. The system was simple and, when used properly, quite effective for controlling spending.

The cash envelope's rule was simple: When an envelope was empty, there was no more spending for that category. Money could be taken from another envelope, but then that category could lack funds. A decision had to be made immediately.

Because most families today are paid by check (and holding cash in the home is not always advisable), a different cash allocation system is usually necessary.

The Family Financial Workbook method—The manual budget method described in this workbook is the simplest, yet most complete, possible. It has the advantage of the cash envelope system, without the disadvantages.

It is important to know how much should be spent, how much is being spent, and how much is left to spend in each budget category. To accomplish this, Individual Account Pages (Form 7) have been substituted for envelopes. All the money is deposited into a checking account, and Individual Account Pages are used to accomplish what the envelopes once accomplished.

Understanding Budget Categories

After tracking your spending by the suggested categories and reviewing the guideline budget, you should already be familiar, generally, with the budget categories. The following expands the explanation of each category.

Gross Income: Include your gross pay for money you earn. Don't forget to include commissions, bonuses, tips, and interest earned that will be received over the next twelve months. Business expense reimbursements should not be considered family income. Avoid the trap of using expense money to buffer family spending or the result will be an indebtedness that cannot be paid.

Net Spendable Income is the portion available for family spending. Remember from the Division-of-Income principle that some of your income does not belong to the family and, therefore, cannot be spent. These include the Tithe and Taxes below.

Category 1–**The Tithe:** Since the term *tithe* means "a tenth," I will assume that you give 10 percent of your total income to God. (For a detailed discussion on the tithe, see the other resources in Chapter 11, such as *Your Finances in Changing Times* by Larry Burkett.)

Category 2–**Taxes:** Deduct federal withholding, Social Security, and state and local taxes from gross income. Self-employed individuals must not forget to set aside money for quarterly prepayments on taxes. Beware of the tendency to treat unpaid tax money as windfall profit.

Other Deductions: Payroll deductions for insurance, credit union savings or debt payments, bonds, stock programs, retirement, and union dues can be handled in either of two ways.

1. Treat them as a deduction from gross income the same as the income taxes.

2. Include them in spendable income and deduct them from the proper category. This is preferred because it provides a more accurate picture of where the money is being spent.

EXAMPLE: A deduction is being made for credit union savings. This amount should be considered as part of income, with an expense shown under Savings for the same amount. This method makes it easier to see the overall effect the deduction has on the family budget.

Category 3–**Housing Expenses:** All monthly expenses necessary to operate the home, including taxes, insurance, maintenance, and utilities. If you cannot establish an accurate maintenance expense, use 5 percent of the monthly mortgage payment as a guideline.

Category 4–**Food Expenses:** All grocery expenses, including paper goods and nonfood products normally purchased at grocery stores, plus milk, bread, and single-item purchases in addition to regular shopping trips. Do not include eating out and daily lunches eaten away from home.

Category 5 **Auto Expenses:** Includes payments, insurance, gas, oil, maintenance, repairs, and depreciation. Depreciation is actually the money set aside to repair or replace the automobile. The minimum amount set aside should be sufficient to keep the car in decent repair and to replace it at least every four to five years. If replacement funds are not available in the budget, a minimum allocation should cover maintenance costs.

Category 6–**Insurance:** Includes insurance not associated with the home or auto: health, life, and disability.

Category 7–**Debts:** Includes all monthly payments required to meet debt obligations. Home mortgage and car payments are not included here.

Category 8–**Entertainment/Recreation:** Vacation savings, camping trips, club dues, sporting equipment, hobby expenses, and athletic events. Don't forget Little League expense, booster clubs, and so on.

Category 9–**Clothing:** Includes clothes, shoes, and coats for all family members.

Category 10–**Savings:** Every family should allocate something for savings. A savings account can provide funds for emergencies and is a key element in good planning and financial freedom.

Category 11–**Medical Expenses:** Includes deductibles, doctors' bills, eyeglasses, prescription drugs, and orthodontist visits.

Category 12–**Miscellaneous:** Specific expenses that do not seem to fit anywhere else, such as gifts, toiletries, haircuts, subscriptions, or postage.

CHAPTER

No person was ever honored for what he received. Honor has been the reward for what he gave.

—Calvin Coolidge

Category 13–**Investments:** Individuals and families with surplus income in their budgets will have the opportunity to invest for retirement or other long-term goals. As debt-free status is achieved, more money can be diverted to this category.

Category 14–**School/Child Care:** Includes child care, tuition, school supplies, and fees for school projects and activities.

Category 15–**Unallocated Surplus Income:** Includes income from unbudgeted sources (garage sales or gifts). It can be kept in one's checking account and placed in this category.

Allocating Income

Although you should focus most of your efforts on expenses, the starting point for your budget is tracking and planning your income. Your first step is to spread, or allocate, your income to various spending categories.

A helpful tool to accomplish this is the Income Allocation page (Form 5). Its purpose is to divide Net Spendable Income among the various budget categories. It is simply a predetermined plan of how each paycheck or income source is going to be spent.

After you have determined how much can be spent in each category per month, write that amount in the Monthly Allocation column.

Next, divide the monthly allocation for each category (Housing, Food, Auto) by pay period.

EXAMPLE: Family income is received twice each month. Note that the mortgage payment is made on the 29th of the month, so the allocation must be divided in a manner to make sure that adequate funds are available at the time the payment is due. Utility and maintenance payments would have to be made from another pay period.

Category	Monthly Allocation	Pay Periods 1.	2.
Housing	$672	$500	$172
Food	$248	$124	$124
Auto	$248	$175	$ 73
Insurance	$ 39	$ 14	$ 25

It is not mandatory that checks be divided evenly. The important thing is to have money available when a payment is due. Therefore, some reserve funds from middle-of-the-month pay periods must be held to meet obligations that come due at the first of the month.

Monitoring Spending

Just as each category had its own envelope under the cash envelope system, each budget category has its own Individual Account Page (Form 7) in this budget system. This approach allows you to view quickly and easily how much is left in each category and for what the monthly allocation has been spent.

At the top of the page, the proper account category title and the monthly allocation are entered (Housing, Food, Automobile). Each account category sheet has two blanks ($\_\_\_\_\_$), where you may use an allocation for a twice-monthly pay period, if you prefer.

INDIVIDUAL ACCOUNT PAGE

_____	$ _____	$ _____
Account Category	Allocation	Allocation

The purpose of the account category sheet is to document all transactions for the month. Show the pay period allocation as a deposit. Show all expenses as withdrawals, and then adjust your category balance after each transaction.

If funds are left at the end of the month, the Individual Account Page is zeroed by transferring the money to the Savings category. If a category runs short, then it may be necessary to transfer money from Savings to the appropriate account. When a category is out of money, a decision must be made concerning how it is going to be treated.

How to Use the Budget System

To help you better understand how to use the budget system, we will examine one category (Housing) and review a typical month's transactions.

Figure 6.1 shows a typical family budget in which the gross income of $2,083 per month is received in two pay periods of $1,041 and $1,042.

I know of no country [America], indeed, where the love of money has taken stronger hold on the affections of men.

—Alexis de Tocqueville

INCOME ALLOCATION

BUDGET CATEGORY	MONTHLY ALLOCATION	1st $1,041	15th $1,042		
1. Tithe	$208	104	104		
2. Tax	106	53	53		
3. Housing	672	500	172		
4. Food	248	124	124		
5. Auto	248	175	73		
6. Insurance	39	14	25		
7. Debts	90				

INDIVIDUAL ACCOUNT PAGE

Housing ③ s 500 s 172

DATE	TRANSACTION	DEPOSIT	WITHDRAWAL	BALANCE
12/1	Allocation	$500 00		$500 00
12/15	Mortgage		$500 00	-0-
12/15	Allocation	172 00		172 00
12/20	Electric		70 00	102 00
12/30	Transfer to Savings		102 00	-0-

Figure 6.1

Pay Allocation—The two checks have been divided as evenly as possible among the necessary categories. For example, the Tithe is paid each pay period (remember it is based on gross income). The housing allocation of $672 is divided, $500 in the first pay period, $172 in the second. For simplicity, in this example other housing expenses, such as utilities, taxes, and insurance are not shown here.

Housing Allocation—On the first pay period, a deposit of $500 is noted on the category page. On the fifteenth, $172 is added, the mortgage is paid and noted as a withdrawal, and the balance is $0.

Each transaction is noted similarly until, at the end of the month, a balance of $61 is left (thanks to a garage sale). This balance is then transferred to Savings, (see Figure 6.2) as are month-end balances from the other category pages (Food, Entertainment). Hence, each category starts at zero the next month.

Many people prefer to leave the surplus funds from each category in their checking accounts, rather than transfer them to a savings account. This is acceptable if you can discipline yourself not to spend the money just because it's easily accessible. Often the total cash reserves in the checking are enough to qualify for free checking privileges, which more than offset any loss of interest in a savings account.

NOTE: In many cases, the Housing category may have to carry a surplus forward to make the mortgage payment if it comes due on the first of the month.

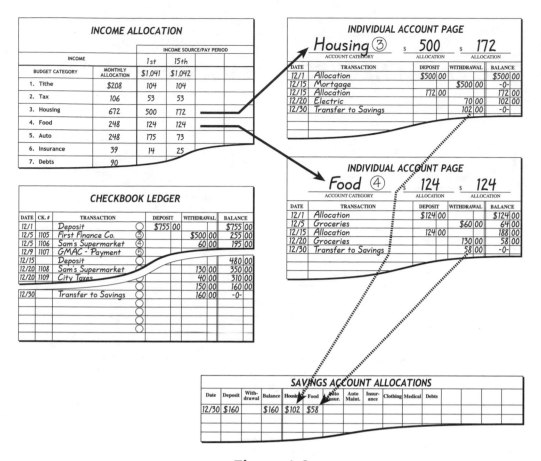

INCOME ALLOCATION

INCOME		INCOME SOURCE/PAY PERIOD	
		1st	15th
BUDGET CATEGORY	MONTHLY ALLOCATION	$1,041	$1,042
1. Tithe	$208	104	104
2. Tax	106	53	53
3. Housing	672	500	172
4. Food	248	124	124
5. Auto	248	175	73
6. Insurance	39	14	25
7. Debts	90		

INDIVIDUAL ACCOUNT PAGE

Housing ③ $ 500 $ 172

DATE	TRANSACTION	DEPOSIT	WITHDRAWAL	BALANCE
12/1	Allocation	$500 00		$500 00
12/15	Mortgage		$500 00	-0-
12/15	Allocation	172 00		172 00
12/20	Electric		70 00	102 00
12/30	Transfer to Savings		102 00	-0-

INDIVIDUAL ACCOUNT PAGE

Food ④ $ 124 $ 124

DATE	TRANSACTION	DEPOSIT	WITHDRAWAL	BALANCE
12/1	Allocation	$124 00		$124 00
12/5	Groceries		$60 00	64 00
12/15	Allocation	124 00		188 00
12/20	Groceries		130 00	58 00
12/30	Transfer to Savings		58 00	-0-

CHECKBOOK LEDGER

DATE	CK. #	TRANSACTION	DEPOSIT	WITHDRAWAL	BALANCE
12/1		Deposit	$755 00		$755 00
12/5	1105	First Finance Co. ③		$500 00	255 00
12/5	1106	Sam's Supermarket ④		60 00	195 00
12/9	1107	GMAC - Payment ⑤			
12/15		Deposit			480 00
12/20	1108	Sam's Supermarket		130 00	350 00
12/20	1109	City Taxes		40 00	310 00
				150 00	160 00
12/30		Transfer to Savings		160 00	-0-

SAVINGS ACCOUNT ALLOCATIONS

Date	Deposit	Withdrawal	Balance	Housing	Food	Auto Insur.	Auto Maint.	Insurance	Clothing	Medical	Debts		
12/30	$160		$160	$102	$58								

Figure 6.2

If you can't pay as you go, you are going too fast.

—Anon

Bookkeeping Tasks

To simplify your bookkeeping, I recommend using a checkbook that gives you a duplicate copy of each check written. It will reduce the number of steps in the bookkeeping process. Develop a way to mark each duplicate copy of your check after you have recorded the check in its appropriate category.

If you prefer, you may use the Checkbook Ledger, Form 7a. You record each deposit and withdrawal and adjust the outstanding balance. At the end of each month, balance the Checkbook Ledger form against the bank statement. See page 60 for "The Easy Checkbook Balance Procedure."

If there are additional deposits or withdrawals from the bank statement recorded in the Checkbook Ledger, you should record them in the appropriate Individual Category pages. For example, a service charge from the bank would be posted as an expense in the Checkbook Ledger and as a miscellaneous expense in category 12 of the budget.

Also, note when you have reconciled the check with your bank statement by placing a

THE EASY CHECKBOOK BALANCE PROCEDURE

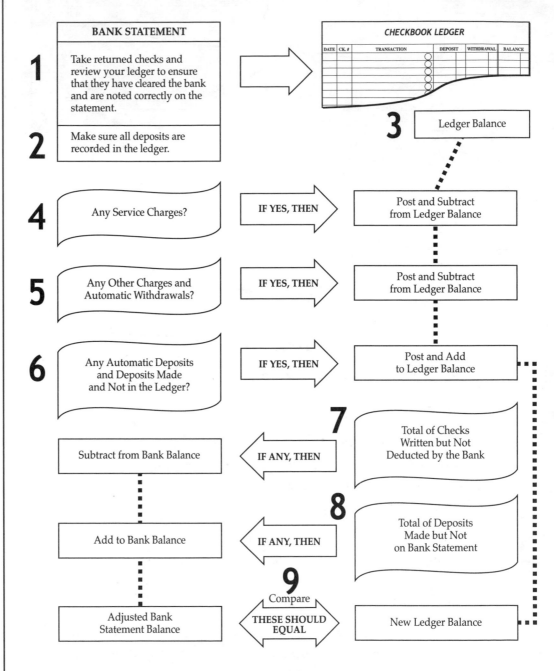

BANK STATEMENT

1 Take returned checks and review your ledger to ensure that they have cleared the bank and are noted correctly on the statement.

2 Make sure all deposits are recorded in the ledger.

CHECKBOOK LEDGER

DATE	CK. #	TRANSACTION	DEPOSIT	WITHDRAWAL	BALANCE

3 Ledger Balance

4 Any Service Charges? → IF YES, THEN → Post and Subtract from Ledger Balance

5 Any Other Charges and Automatic Withdrawals? → IF YES, THEN → Post and Subtract from Ledger Balance

6 Any Automatic Deposits and Deposits Made and Not in the Ledger? → IF YES, THEN → Post and Add to Ledger Balance

7 Total of Checks Written but Not Deducted by the Bank → IF ANY, THEN → Subtract from Bank Balance

8 Total of Deposits Made but Not on Bank Statement → IF ANY, THEN → Add to Bank Balance

Adjusted Bank Statement Balance

9 Compare THESE SHOULD EQUAL

New Ledger Balance

Figure 6.3

check by the transaction on Form 7a. This tells you whether that check has been reconciled with the bank statement.

It is common practice with many budgeters to write the checks, record (post) the checks in the Checkbook Ledger (Figure 6.4), and then record the transactions in the Individual Account Pages at a later time. To ensure that all checks are recorded on the Individual Account sheets, a notation of the category number should be made for each entry in the Checkbook Ledger in the appropriate block.

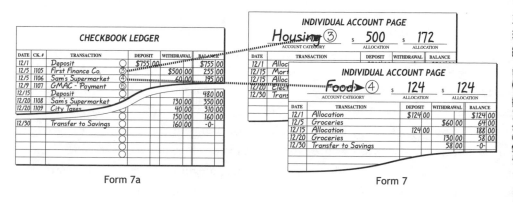

Figure 6.4

The Individual Account Pages ("envelopes") keep track of money in the checking account. The Savings Account Allocation page keeps track of money in the Savings category (Figure 6.2). However, you may want to use a Savings Category page (or envelope) within the checking account to minimize transfers to and from the savings account.

Remember, the plan is to know what each dollar in the checking account is for and what each dollar in the savings account is for. When you spend money, you need to know which money is spent (Clothing, Food, Auto, or others).

Reaching a Danger Point

Your budget may reveal that you are at the danger point when income barely equals outgo. Breaking even is not a living point; it is a deciding point. If all the income is consumed in monthly expenses and something unusual happens, such as the family vehicle breaking down, the result is additional indebtedness.

The necessary decision at this point is to *make more money or spend less.*

Ideally, this decision should be made before external pressures leave few alternatives. Unfortunately, when the pressure comes on, the credit card comes out. The result is a debt that cannot be paid. That limits the alternatives to treating the "symptoms."

Some typical treatments are bill consolidation loans, additional credit, second mort-gages, or work outside the home for the stay-at-home mother. Those may provide temporary relief, but, because only the symptom has been treated, the problem still exists. It's only a matter of time until symptoms reappear.

You should not blame your budget or give up budgeting at this point. Use the budget as a tool to move away from the danger point. Cut expenses, perhaps increase income by taking on a second job temporarily, or sell assets. Get committed and get serious to moving your family away from danger.

Handling a Good Problem: Surplus Income

I have found, in using the budget system myself, that sometimes I have more money than I budgeted. I could simply have transferred it to my Savings category and often did so if the money was to be used several months later. But if the money was going to be used within a few weeks, I wanted to leave it in the checking account. Since I did not want it allocated to any of the regular monthly categories, I created a fifteenth cat-egory just to hold these surplus funds. This allowed me to keep each of the other cate-gories constant each month. You may find this system helpful if you periodically have extra income that is unallocated.

The Final Word

No technique, no matter how simple or complicated, will make your budget work. In order to make your budget work, you have to discipline yourself. You must discipline yourself to spend money based on the bottom line of each category and not based on the bottom line of the checkbook.

Living Proof Testimony

A debt-free, stay-at-home mom began listening to the "Money Matters" radio program ten years ago. After six months of marriage, she and her husband were broke. They started on a budget.

"Yes, there have been 'sacrifices,' like having one car, using cloth diapers, and buying nearly everything second-hand. But it's worth it! We feel so blessed to have God working His will in our lives and look forward to seeing HIM continue to meet our needs."

BUDGET
CHALLENGES

If a person gets his attitude toward money straight, it will help straighten out almost every other area in his life.
                                                            –Billy Graham

BUDGET CHALLENGES

So far, you have learned the many reasons to start and keep a budget. This workbook shows you a straightforward, manual budget system. Even though it has many benefits and is not difficult, there are some challenges to keeping a budget–just like the challenges of staying fit or praying regularly.

If keeping a budget required no discipline, no effort, no tough dilemmas, no change of habits, then everyone would be doing it.

This chapter will equip you and give you helpful tools for the areas of budgeting that challenge people the most.

- Cash withdrawals
- Variable and contingent expenses
- Variable income
- Impulse buying
- Gifts
- Bookkeeping errors
- Attitude challenges
- Other challenges

Cash or ATM Withdrawals

Cash withdrawals are not bad themselves, but the danger is that they never get recorded in your budget. Then, your categories do not reflect actual spending.

The actual withdrawal of cash should be recorded in your Checkbook Ledger (Form 7a). It should not yet be recorded on an Individual Account Page, because you have not spent money yet.

Let's say that you spend cash regularly for lunches and snacks at work, for gas, and for the occasional quick grocery stop. Record these cash expenses in your budget on the Individual Account Page, just as you would expenses paid by check. Here are some hints for recording these expenses.

1. Keep receipts from cash transactions. Use the receipts as reminders to record

them, *or*

2. Keep a separate cash diary in which you note your cash expenses during the day. Then, you transfer those to the appropriate category, *or*

3. Use cash envelopes and separate personal cash into categories identical to the account pages. For this approach, record the expense in the Individual Account Page when the cash is set aside. For example, you put $20 in the Gas envelope to carry with you for cash expenditures. Record the $20 expenditure at the time you withdraw the cash. Avoid spending gas money for lunches and grocery money for entertainment.

Budgeting for Variable and Contingent Expenses

	Estimated Cost			Per Month
1. Vacation	$ _____	÷ 12 =	$ _____
2. Dentist	$ _____	÷ 12 =	$ _____
3. Doctor	$ __240__	÷ 12 =	$ __20__
4. Auto	$ __480__	÷ 12 =	$ __40__
5. Annual Insurance	$ _____	÷ 12 =	$ _____
(Life)	($ _____	÷ 12 =	$ _____)
(Health)	($ _____	÷ 12 =	$ _____)
(Auto)	($ __720__	÷ 12 =	$ __60__)
(Home)	($ _____	÷ 12 =	$ _____)
6. Clothing	$ __600__	÷ 12 =	$ __50__
7. Investments	$ _____	÷ 12 =	$ _____
8. Other	$ _____	÷ 12 =	$ _____
	$ _____	÷ 12 =	$ _____

Figure 7.1

You have set up your budget on a monthly basis, but not all expenses occur on a monthly basis. You know that you will have expenses in any given year for auto maintenance, medical bills, or home repairs.

You must budget for these expenses and set aside, or reserve, any money not spent in a particular month for these items. Without the needed reserves, the result is often additional debt when those expenses occur.

Use Form 2, Variable Expense Planning, to estimate the annual expenses for any variable categories. After you decide what is needed for the next year, divide the amount by twelve to determine what must be saved on a monthly basis. Include these amounts in the proper categories when planning the total budget. See Figure 7.1.

Items such as automobiles, appliances, and household goods (furniture, tools, rugs) wear out or deteriorate over time. You should include replacement of these items in your budget allocation.

The dangerous tendency in tight budgeting situations is to avoid maintenance and depreciation savings with the excuse that you "just can't afford it." Even if the full amount cannot be set aside, try to save something for those purposes. Depreciation is the same as any other expense. Without money to repair a car, the usual alternative is to replace it—on the debt payment plan!

Failure to plan for short-range variables and depreciating items results in crisis planning. Control your expenditures; don't let them control you.

At the end of each month, the allocated money not actually used is transferred to a savings account. Refer to the illustration below where the savings ledger shows the surplus by budget category.

SAVINGS ACCOUNT ALLOCATIONS													
Date	Deposit	With-drawal	Balance	Housing	Food	Auto Insur.	Auto Maint.	Insur-ance	Clothing	Medical	Debts		
12/30	$160		$160	$102	$58								

Figure 7.2

Here are additional hints to help with budgeting for variable expenses.

- **Convert variable expenses to constant expenses.** Many utility companies offer "budget billing" if your bill is constant each month. Signing up for this service is an example of changing fluctuating expenses to a constant amount. Instead of paying insurance semiannually or quarterly, try to pay monthly (if the service charges are reasonable). Save automatically each month for vacation or Christmas gifts in savings accounts at your bank or credit union.

- **Be flexible.** In starting a budget, it may be necessary to borrow from one account to supplement another. For example, if the car breaks down before a surplus is accumulated in the Auto account, it may be necessary to borrow from Clothing or Medical surpluses to pay for the car repair. However, to continue to do that month after month will defeat the long-range purpose in budgeting. That purpose is to plan ahead!

Budgeting on a Variable Income

One of the most difficult problems in budgeting is how to allocate monthly spending when your income fluctuates, as it often does on commission sales. The normal tendency is to spend the money as it comes in. This works great during the high-income months but usually causes havoc during lower-income months.

Two suggestions will help anyone living on a fluctuating income.

- First, always separate any business-related expenses, such as car maintenance, meals, or living accommodations, from your normal household expenses. I recommend a separate checking account for business expenses and separate credit cards, if needed.

CHAPTER 7

Our economy is based upon people wanting more–their happiness on wanting less.

–Frank A. Clark

- Second, you need to estimate what your (low) average income for one year will be and generate your monthly budget based on the "average" income per month. As the funds come in, deposit them in a special savings account and draw the average monthly salary from the account. The effect is to ration the income over the year in relatively equal amounts that can be budgeted.

Remember, if you are self-employed, you will need to budget for taxes on a quarterly basis. Failure to do this will result in a rather unpleasant visit with the representatives of the Internal Revenue Service.

If you are beginning your budget during one of the lower income months, you may have to delay funding some of the variable expense categories such as clothing, vacations, or dental. These can be funded later when the income allows.

Impulse Buying

Impulse items are unnecessary spur-of-the-moment purchases. Purchases of impulse items usually result in overspending, additional debt, and family arguments.

The purchases are usually rationalized by the following phrases.

- "It was on sale."
- "I was planning to buy it anyway."
- "I've always wanted one."
- "I may use it as a gift."
- "The store offered a great financing plan."
- "I just couldn't resist it."
- "I deserve it."

Often, impulse purchases are made with a credit card because the cash isn't available. The net result is little-used items and unnecessary debt.

"Impulse purchases" are not restricted to small items. They range from unscheduled restaurant meals to cars and homes. Cost is not the issue; necessity is. Every purchase should be considered in light of the budget.

Discipline is the key to controlling impulse buying. As a helpful tool, use the "Impulse List" suggested in the Motivational Reminders tear-out at the end of the chapter.

Establish the discipline that before buying on impulse you will list the item on the Impulse List, talk about it with your spouse, obtain comparison prices, and wait thirty days before purchasing the item.

If you feel you still need the item at the end of the thirty days and the money is available, then buy it. You will eliminate most impulse items by this discipline. Here's an example of how it works.

IMPULSE LIST					
Date	Impulse Item	Price 1	Price 2	Price 3	Category
9/28	Pop-up Camper	$2,000			Vacation
10/12	New set of golf clubs	$675	$600		Recreation
10/16	Porcelain figurine collection	$150			Miscellaneous

Figure 7.3

Gifts

A major budget-buster in most families is overspending on gifts. Unless you keep a budget, it would likely surprise you what you spend on birthdays (including the parties your kids attend), wedding and shower gifts, anniversaries, Father's and Mother's Day, gifts for kids' teachers, coworkers' gifts, and Christmas gifts.

Tradition dictates a gift for nearly every occasion. Unfortunately, the net result is often a gift someone else doesn't want, purchased with money that was needed for something else. Many times the cost increases because the gift is selected at the last moment. If gifts are a part of normal spending, budget for them and buy ahead—reasonably.

To bring the cost of gifts under control, consider the following hints.
• Keep an event calendar for the year.
• Plan ahead and shop wisely. For example, buy fall/winter items on sale in the early spring to give as Christmas gifts later in the year.
• Determine not to buy any gifts on credit (especially Christmas gifts).
• Initiate crafts within the family and make some gifts.
• Give meaningful service or "time-with-you" coupons (baby-sitting, fishing outing, or two hours of yard work) instead of store-bought items.
• Draw family names for selected gifts rather than giving to everyone.

CHAPTER

Every man has the secret of becoming rich who resolves to live within his means.

—Anon

Budget Challenges

Bookkeeping Errors

Common sources of bookkeeping errors include failing to record a check in your ledger or in your budget, failing to record a credit card transaction, or making mathematical errors.

An accurately balanced checkbook is a must. Even small errors result in big problems if they are allowed to compound. An inaccurate balance can result in an overdrawn account, as well as in significant bank charges. See the example of the The Easy Checkbook Balance Procedure form on page 60.

Direct deposits into checking accounts also must be noted in the home ledger at the proper time. Don't forget to include bank service charges in the home ledger.

The following is a list of tips for keeping good records.

- **Use a ledger type checkbook rather than a stub type.** The ledger gives greater visibility and lends itself to fewer errors. I recommend using a checkbook that has a duplicate copy of the checks written. This eliminates errors in not posting a check.

- **Be certain all checks are accounted for.** All checks should be entered in the ledger when written. This entry must include the check number, amount, date, and assignee. Tearing checks out of your checkbook for future use defeats many of the safeguards built into this system. I recommend that all checks be written only from the checkbook.

- **Remember to account for automatic deductions from your checking account.** Automatic payment deductions must be subtracted from the checkbook ledger at the time they are paid by the bank. For example, an insurance premium is paid by automatic withdrawal on the fifteenth of each month. You must make certain that on the fifteenth of every month the proper amount is deducted from your home checking account records.

- **Assign one person as the primary bookkeeper.** Both the husband and the wife should be involved in setting and reviewing the budget. However, most budgets tend to work best with one individual maintaining the detail records. The choice should be based on who can do the job best.

- **Maintain a home ledger.** If all records are kept in a checkbook ledger, you run the risk of losing it. A home ledger eliminates this possibility and makes record keeping more orderly. Use Form 7a in the forms section as your Checkbook Ledger sheet.

- **Balance the checking account (and any credit card statements) every month—to the penny.** Never allow the home ledger and bank statement to disagree in balance. The two most common errors are math errors (addition or subtraction) and transposition errors (writing in the wrong amount). Use a calculator and balance the account.

Attitude Challenges

Impatience. In our fast-paced society, it's hard to be patient. Solving your financial problems may take as long or even longer than it took for them to develop.

Discouragement. Changing habits is never easy. You may overspend and mess up your budget at the beginning, but you can learn and move forward. Others have done it and you can too.

Legalism. Another problem is becoming legalistic and inflexible. The budget can become a family weapon instead of a family tool. Becoming legalistic, incidentally, seems to occur at the same time the money runs out. Remain flexible to necessary changes.

Overcorrection and Blame. When the money gets tight, the tendency is to eliminate clothing, entertainment, food, and other "expendables." That creates a pressure that is often relieved by overspending in other areas.

Other Budget Challenges

Mixing or Splitting Categories. Don't try to make the record keeping more complicated than necessary. For example, you go to the grocery store to buy your weekly food items, but you also buy toilet paper and aspirin. Because the majority of the purchase is food, go ahead and record the expense to food instead of food, miscellaneous, and medical. After you become more adept at budgeting, then you can divide one expense or receipt among several categories.

Try to not develop any more detailed categories than the fourteen categories presented in Chapter 6. The goal is to achieve progress, not perfection. If you choose to develop more detailed breakdowns of expenses and savings, wait until the budget has been in use at least for six months.

Biweekly Payroll. If you happen to be one of those families paid every two weeks rather than twice monthly, you will have two extra paychecks a year. I recommend using those paychecks to fund some of the non-monthly expenses, such as car repair, vacation, and clothing. The same is true of tax refunds, bonuses, and gifts.

Automatic Overdraft Protection. Many banks offer an automatic overdraft protection service. Thus, if you write a check in excess of what you have in your account, the bank will still honor it. On the surface this looks like a helpful service. However, it has been my experience that overdraft protection tends to create a complacent attitude about balancing the account and encourages overdrafts. Because these charges are accrued to a credit account, you will end up paying interest on your overdrafts. I recommend that these services be avoided until the budgeting routine is well established.

Motivational Reminders

Carry your Impulse List in your purse or wallet. Establish the discipline that before buying on impulse you will list the item on the impulse list, talk about it with your spouse, obtain comparison prices, and wait thirty days before purchasing the item.

IMPULSE LIST

Date	Impulse Item	Price 1	Price 2	Price 3	Category

In Chapter 10, the forms section, you will find an Impulse List (Form 9), which you can tear out and copy for your own use.

Living Proof Testimony

When a woman began listening to "Money Matters" seven years ago, her husband was not a Christian. When she heard the radio program for the first time, they were paying thirty-six bills monthly. She told her husband she wanted to tithe on her income. She did and he watched what happened. Six months later he said, "Just pay on mine too!" Three months later he started going to church with her, and he accepted the Lord as his Savior.

"We've gone from paying 36 bills a month, to 5 bills a month, and one of those is the tithe. Life is so much better with God in the pilot's chair!"

CHAPTER

A purse is doubly empty when it is full of borrowed money.

—Anon

RESOURCE SECTION: MONEY-SAVING TIPS

If you would be wealthy, think of saving rather than getting. —Benjamin Franklin

RESOURCE SECTION: MONEY-SAVING TIPS

Food

Many families buy too much food. Others buy too little. Typically, the average American family buys the wrong type of food. The reduction of a family's food bill requires quantity and quality planning.

Grocery Shopping Hints

1. Always use a written list of needs.

2. Try to conserve gas by buying food for a longer time period and in larger quantities.

3. Avoid buying when hungry (especially if you're a "sugarholic").

4. Use a calculator, if possible, to total purchases. Reduce or eliminate paper products: paper plates, cups, napkins (use cloth napkins).

5. Evaluate where to purchase sundry items, such as shampoo, mouthwash. (These are normally somewhat cheaper at discount stores.)

6. Avoid processed and sugarcoated cereals. (These are expensive and most of them have little nutritional value.)

7. Avoid prepared foods, such as frozen dinners, pot pies, cakes. (You are paying for expensive labor that you can provide.)

8. Determine good meat cuts that are available from roasts or shoulders, and have the butcher cut these for you. (Buying steaks by the package on sale is fairly inexpensive also.)

9. Try store brand canned products. (These are normally cheaper and just as nutritious.)

10. Avoid products in a seasonal price hike. Substitute or eliminate.

11. Shop for advertised specials. (These are usually posted in the store window.)

12. Use manufacturer's coupons (cents-off on an item or items) only if you were going to buy the item anyway and it is cheaper than another brand would be without the coupon.

13. When possible, purchase food in bulk quantities from large discount stores; the per-item cost is cheaper. Do not buy from convenience stores except in case of emergency.

14. Avoid buying non-grocery items in a grocery supermarket except on sale. (These are normally "high mark-up" items.)

15. For baby foods, use normal foods processed in a blender.

16. Leave the children at home to avoid unnecessary pressure.

17. Check every item as it is being "rung up" at the store and again when you get home.

18. Consider canning fresh vegetables whenever possible. Make bulk purchases with other families at farmers' markets and such. (Note: Buy canning supplies during off-seasons.)

Automobiles

Many families will buy new cars they can't afford and trade them long before their utility is depleted. Those who buy a new car, keep it for less than four years, and then trade it for a new model have wasted the maximum amount of money. Some people, such as salespeople that drive a great deal, need new cars frequently; most of us don't. We swap cars because we want to—not because we have to. Many factors are involved, such as ego, esteem, and maturity.

Leasing often seems to be a good alternative because it requires little initial cash outlay. However, a lease is a long-term financial commitment that many families cannot afford. Remember, when you buy something you can't afford, leasing doesn't avoid the decision; it only delays it.

Insurance

It is unfortunate to see so many families misled in this area. Few people understand insurance, either how much is needed or what kind is necessary. Who would be foolish enough to buy a Rolls Royce when he or she could afford only a Chevrolet? Yet many purchase high-cost insurance even though their needs dictate otherwise.

Insurance should be used as supplementary provision for the family, not protection or profit. An insurance plan is not designed for saving money or for retirement. Ask anyone who assumed it was; the ultimate result was disillusionment and disappointment.

In our society, insurance can be used as an inexpensive vehicle to provide future family income and thus release funds today for family use and the Lord's work. In excess, this same insurance can put a family in debt, steal the Lord's money, and transfer dependence to the world.

One of your best insurance assets is to have a trustworthy agent in charge of your program. A good insurance agent is usually one who can select from several different companies to provide you with the best possible buy and who will create a brief, uncomplicated plan to analyze your exact needs.

Debts

It would be great if most budgets included 5 percent debts or less. Unfortunately, the norm in American families is far in excess of this amount. As previously discussed, credit cards, bank loans, and installment credit have made it possible for families to go deeply into debt. What things can you do if this situation exists?

• Destroy all credit cards as a first step.

• Establish a payment schedule that includes all creditors.

• Contact all creditors, honestly relate your problems, and arrange an equitable repayment plan.

• Buy on a cash basis, and sacrifice your wants and desires until you are current.

Recreation/Entertainment

We are a recreation-oriented country. That isn't necessarily bad if put in the proper perspective; however, those who're in debt cannot use their creditor's money to entertain themselves. The normal tendency is to escape problems, even if only for a short while—even if the problems then become more acute. Christians must resist this urge and control recreation and entertainment expenses while in debt.

What a terrible witness it is for a Christian who is already in financial bondage to indulge at the expense of others. God knows we need rest and relaxation, and He will often provide it from unexpected sources, once our attitudes are correct. Every believer, whether in debt or not, should seek to reduce entertainment expenses. This usually can be done without sacrificing quality family time.

CHAPTER

I care for riches, to make gifts to friends, or lead a sick man back to health with ease and plenty. Else small aid is wealth for daily gladness.

–Euripides

Recreation Hints

1. Plan vacations during "off seasons" if possible.

2. Consider a camping vacation to avoid motel and food expenses. (Christian friends can pool the expenses of camping items.)

3. Select vacation areas in your general locale. Use some family games in place of movies (like some of those unused games received at Christmas).

4. Consider two or more families taking vacation trips together to reduce expenses and increase fellowship.

5. If flying, use the least expensive coach fare (i.e., late night or early morning usually saves 10 percent to 20 percent).

Clothing

Many families in debt sacrifice this area in their budget because of excesses in other areas. And yet, with prudent planning and buying your family can be clothed neatly without great expense. This requires effort on your part to do the following.

*   Save enough money to buy without using credit.

*   Educate family members on care of clothing.

*   Apply discipline with children to enforce these habits.

*   Develop skills in making and mending clothing.

Learn to be utilizers of resources rather than consumers. How many families have closets full of clothes they no longer wear because they are out of style?

Many families with large surplus incomes spend excessively in the area of clothing. Assess whether it really matters that you have all of the latest styles. Instead, do your purchases reflect good utility, rather than ego? Do you buy clothes to satisfy a need or a desire?

Budget Hints

1. Make as many of the clothes as time will allow. (Average savings are 50 percent to 60 percent.)

2. Make a written list of clothing needs and purchase during the off season when possible.

3. Select outfits that can be mixed and used in multiple combinations rather than as a single set.

4. Frequent the discount outlets that carry unmarked name brand goods.

5. Frequent authentic factory outlet stores for close-out values of top quality.

6. Select clothing made of home washable fabrics. Use coin-operated dry cleaning machines instead of commercial cleaners.

7. Practice early repair for damaged clothing.

8. Learn to utilize all clothing fully (especially children's wear).

He that goes a borrowing goes a sorrowing.

–Benjamin Franklin

Savings

It is important that some savings be included in the budget. Otherwise, the use of credit becomes a lifelong necessity and debt a way of life. Your savings will allow you to purchase items for cash and shop for the best buys.

Savings Hints

1. Use a company payroll withdrawal, if possible. This removes the money before you receive it.

2. Use an automatic bank withdrawal from your checking account.

3. Write your savings account a check just as if it were a creditor.

4. When an existing debt is paid off, allocate any extra money toward the next largest debt. When all consumer debt is paid off, then reallocate that money to savings.

Medical/Dental expenses

You must anticipate these expenses in your budget and set aside funds regularly; failure to do so will wreck your plans and lead to indebtedness. Do not sacrifice family health due to lack of planning; but, at the same time, do not use doctors excessively.

Proper prevention is much cheaper than correction. You can avoid many dental bills by teaching children to eat the right foods and clean their teeth properly. Your dentist will supply all the information you need on this subject. Many doctor bills can be avoided in the same way. Take proper care of your body through diet, rest, and exercise, and it will respond with good health. Abuse your body and you must ultimately pay through illnesses and malfunctions. This is not to say that all illnesses or problems are caused by neglect, but a great many are.

Do not be hesitant to question doctors and dentists in advance about costs. Also, educate yourself enough to discern when you are getting good value for your money. Most ethical professionals will not take offense at your questions. If they do, that may be a hint to change services.

In the case of prescriptions, shop around. You will be amazed to discover the wide variance in prices from one store to the next. Ask about generic drugs. These are usually much less expensive and are just as effective.

Miscellaneous (variable household expenses)

These can include a myriad of items. Some of the expenses occur monthly and others occur on an as-needed basis (such as repairs).

Some merchants will give 5 to 10 percent discounts for cash purchases of major items, such as cars or appliances, and also many gas stations provide the same cash discount.

One of the most important factors in home expenses is you. If you can perform routine maintenance and repair, considerable expenses can be avoided. Many people rationalize not doing these things on the basis that time is too valuable. That is nonsense. If every hour of the day is tied up in the pursuit of money, as previously defined, then you're in bondage. A part of care and maintenance around the home relates to family life, particularly the training of children. When they see mom and dad willing to do some physical labor to help around the home, they will learn good habits. But if you refuse to get involved, why should they? Where will they ever learn the skills of self-sufficiency?

Some men avoid working on home projects because they say they lack the necessary skills. Well, those skills are learned, and there are many good books that detail every area of home maintenance. As previously mentioned, at some point in the future many of these skills will be necessities rather than choices.

Investments

Individuals and families with surplus income in their budgets will have the opportunity to invest for retirement or other long-term goals. As debt-free status is achieved, more money can be diverted to this category.

Living Proof Testimonies

This woman writes how they have learned and practiced biblical principles of finance. It has allowed them to pay off their home five years after they bought it, and they live on one income so she can be a stay-at-home mother.

"*[We have]* one car, use cloth diapers, and buy nearly everything second-hand."

The love of money is a root of all sorts of evil, and some by longing for it have wandered away from the faith and pierced themselves with many griefs.

–the apostle Paul in 1Timothy 6:10

* * *

Even though it's rather uncommon for a family with six children and one income to make it financially these days, here's one that does just that, and has a bonus as well.

"We have six children, one income, older furniture, and drive older vehicles ('86 and '87). We have an above ground swimming pool. We don't take elaborate vacations. For many years we went to a Christian family camp. It was very cost effective and lots of fun for the whole family. And, of course, we're debt free."

* * *

After losing a job, this couple did without movies and eating out, They had a good alternative.

"We did activities with minimal cost like hiking and cooking out."

* * *

This divorced woman learned a low-cost way to have an active social life with her friends.

"When friends invite me to dine out (Dutch treat) I eat before meeting them at the restaurant. I enjoy an appetizer, salad, or dessert. This way the cost is reduced but I am still able to enjoy the fellowship and not feel deprived."

CHAPTER 9

FINANCIAL
RESOURCES
AND TOOLS

If you are not generous with a meager income, you will never be generous with abundance.
—Harold Nye

FINANCIAL RESOURCES AND TOOLS

At this point, you have the necessary tools to establish your own budget. Only one additional ingredient is necessary: desire. No budget will implement itself; it requires effort and good family communication.

Living on a budget is not only prudent; it can be fun. As you have successes in various areas, share them with others. Challenge your children as well. Establish budget goals for them and rewards for achievement.

You'll Find More Help in the Following Resources
Available from Crown Financial Ministries

(Note: Unless otherwise indicated, all items listed are books.)

ATTITUDES

Business by the Book
Crisis Control in the New Millennium
How Much Is Enough?
How Much Is Enough? (video)
Investing for the Future
Using Your Money Wisely
The WORD on Finances (topically arranged Scriptures and commentary)

BORROWING AND DEBT

Bill Organizer (expanding file, audio)
Business by the Book
Complete Financial Guide for Young Couples
Debt-Free Living
God's Principles for Operating a Business (audio)
Great Is Thy Faithfulness (devotional for 365 days)
How to Manage Your Money workbook
Investing for the Future

Money Management for College Students workbook
Money Matters: Answers to Your Financial Questions
Money Matters (software and manual) *Deluxe*
SnapShot Gold™ *CD-ROM* (software)
The WORD on Finances (topically arranged Scriptures and commentary)
Using Your Money Wisely
"World's Easiest Guide" to Finances
Your Finances in Changing Times

BUDGETING

Cash Organizer (spiral-bound envelope system)
How Much Is Enough?
How Much Is Enough? (video)
How to Manage Your Money workbook
Money in Marriage (workbook, CD-ROM, audio)
Money Matters: Answers to Your Financial Questions
Money Matters (software and manual) *Deluxe*
Using Your Money Wisely
The WORD on Finances (topically arranged Scriptures and commentary)
"World's Easiest Guide" to Finances
Your Finances in Changing Times

BUYING AND SELLING

Business by the Book
Complete Financial Guide for Young Couples
Crisis Control in the New Millennium
How Much Is Enough?
How Much Is Enough? (video)
How to Manage Your Money (audio)
Investing for the Future
Money in Marriage (workbook, CD-ROM, audio)
Money Matters: Answers to Your Financial Questions
Money Matters (software and manual) *Deluxe*
SnapShot Gold™ *CD-ROM* (software)
Using Your Money Wisely
The WORD on Finances (topically arranged Scriptures and commentary)

GAMES

Larry Burkett's Money Matters™, *The Christian Financial Concepts board game*
  (ages 10 to adult)
Money Matters for Kids board game (ages 5 to 10)
My Giving Bank (children's bank)

GIVING

Business by the Book
Great Is Thy Faithfulness
How Much Is Enough?
How Much Is Enough? (video)
How to Manage Your Money workbook (audio)
Money in Marriage (workbook, CD-ROM, audio)
Money Matters: Answers to Your Financial Questions
Money Matters (software and manual) *Deluxe*
Two Masters (video)
Using Your Money Wisely
Window of Wisdom™ *CD-ROM Scripture* (software)
The WORD on Finances (topically arranged Scriptures and commentary)
"World's Easiest Guide" to Finances
Your Child Wonderfully Made
Your Finances in Changing Times

HUSBAND'S AND WIFE'S RESPONSIBILITIES

Business by the Book
Career Direct—Occupational (adult guidance system, CD-ROM or paper)
Complete Financial Guide for Young Couples
How Much Is Enough?
How Much Is Enough? (video)
Money in Marriage (workbook, CD ROM, audio)
Money Matters: Answers to Your Financial Questions
Money Matters (software and manual) *Deluxe*
Two Masters (video)
"World's Easiest Guide" to Finances
Using Your Money Wisely

INHERITANCE AND WILLS

Crisis Control in the New Millennium
How to Manage Your Money workbook
Money Matters: Answers to Your Financial Questions
Using Your Money Wisely
Will Kit
The WORD on Finances (topically arranged Scriptures and commentary)
"World's Easiest Guide" to Finances
Your Finances in Changing Times

CHAPTER 9

The love of wealth is therefore to be traced, as either a principle or accessory motive, at the bottom of all that the Americans do.

–Alexis de Tocqueville

Financial Resources and Tools

INVESTMENT AND SAVINGS

Crisis Control in the New Millennium
Debt-Free Living (with *SnapShot Gold* CD-ROM)
How Much Is Enough?
How Much Is Enough? (video)
How to Manage Your Money (workbook, audio, or video)
Investing for the Future
Money Matters: Answers to Your Financial Questions
Money Matters (software and manual) *Deluxe*
Using Your Money Wisely
The WORD on Finances (topically arranged Scriptures and commentary)
"World's Easiest Guide" to Finances

LENDING

Business by the Book
Debt-Free Living
Using Your Money Wisely
The WORD on Finances (topically arranged Scriptures and commentary)

MONEY AND YOUTH

Business by the Book
Career Direct—Educational (student guidance system, CD-ROM or paper)
Cash Organizer (spiral-bound envelope system)
Complete Financial Guide for Young Couples
Consumer Books for College Students
 Buying Your First Car
 Getting Your First Credit Card
 Preparing for College
 Renting Your First Apartment
Crisis Control in the New Millennium
Debt-Free Living
50 Money Making Ideas for Kids
Financial Parenting
Get a Grip on Your Money (ages 16 to 21)
Great Smoky Mountains Storybook Series (ages 5-10)
 A Different Kind of Party
 A Home for the Hamster
 Last Chance for Camp
 Sarah and the Art Contest

How Much Is Enough?
How Much Is Enough? (video)
How to Manage Your Money (workbook, audio, or video)
Making Ends Meet
Money in Marriage (workbook with CD-ROM, audio)
Money Management for College Students
Money Matters: Answers to Your Financial Questions
Money Matters Family Night Tool Chest workbook
Money Matters for Teens workbook (ages 11-14)
Money Matters for Teens workbook (ages 15-18)
My Giving Bank (bank)
105 Questions Children Ask About Money Matters
Surviving the Money Jungle
Using Your Money Wisely
What If I Owned Everything? (ages 3-8)
The WORD on Finances (topically arranged Scriptures and commentary)

RETIREMENT

Crisis Control in the New Millennium
Debt-Free Living
Financial Planning Workshop (audio)
Finding the Career That Fits You workbook
Great Is Thy Faithfulness
How Much Is Enough?
How Much Is Enough? (video)
How to Manage Your Money workbook (audio)
Investing for the Future
Money Matters: Answers to Your Financial Questions
Money Matters (software and manual) *Deluxe*
Using Your Money Wisely

SINGLES' FINANCES

Business by the Book
Career Direct—Educational (student guidance system, CD-ROM or paper)
Complete Financial Guide for Single Parents
Crisis Control in the New Millennium
Debt-Free Living
Every Single Cent (singles without children)
Financial Guide for the Single Parent

Much ingenuity with a little money is vastly more profitable and amusing than much money without ingenuity.

–Arnold Bennett

Financial Guide for the Single Parent workbook
Great Is Thy Faithfulness (devotional for 365 days)
How Much Is Enough?
How Much Is Enough? (video)
How to Manage Your Money workbook (audio)
Investing for the Future
Making Ends Meet
Money Matters 2000 (software and manual)
Using Your Money Wisely
Window of Wisdom CD-ROM (software)
Women Leaving the Workplace

VOCATIONAL DECISIONS

Career Direct—Educational (student guidance system, CD-ROM or paper)
Career Direct—Occupational (adult guidance system, CD-ROM or paper)
Career Direct—YES!™ (Youth Exploration Survey–guidance system, paper format only)
Finding the Career That Fits You workbook
Guide to College Majors and Career Choices
Money Matters: Answers to Your Financial Questions
The PathFinder
Personality I.D.® (adult DISC assessment—paper or Internet version—www.cfcministry.org)
Your Career in Changing Times
The WORD on Finances (topically arranged Scriptures and commentary)

OTHER BOOKS BY LARRY BURKETT

Great Is Thy Faithfulness (devotional book for 365 days)
Hope When It Hurts (about catastrophic illness)

Fiction: *The Illuminati*
        Kingdom Come (with Davis Bunn)
        Solar Flare
        The THOR Conspiracy

For further information about any of these resources or others, contact Crown Financial Ministries, PO Box 2377, Gainesville GA 30503-2377, telephone (770) 534-1000 or (800) 722-1976 or visit us on the Web at www.crown.org.

CHAPTER 10

FORMS

To live content with small means; to seek elegance rather than luxury...to be worthy...wealthy, not rich....This is to be my symphony.

—William Henry Channing

MONTHLY INCOME AND EXPENSES

GROSS INCOME PER MONTH _____

   Salary _____
   Interest _____
   Dividends _____
   Other (_____) _____
   Other (_____) _____

LESS:

1. **Tithe** _____

2. **Tax** (Est.-Incl. Fed., State, FICA) _____

   NET SPENDABLE INCOME _____

3. **Housing** _____
   Mortgage (rent) _____
   Insurance _____
   Taxes _____
   Electricity _____
   Gas _____
   Water _____
   Sanitation _____
   Telephone _____
   Maintenance _____
   Other (_____) _____
   Other (_____) _____

4. **Food** _____

5. **Automobile(s)** _____
   Payments _____
   Gas and Oil _____
   Insurance _____
   License/Taxes _____
   Maint./Repair/Replace _____

6. **Insurance** _____
   Life _____
   Medical _____
   Other (_____) _____

7. **Debts** _____
   Credit Card _____
   Loans and Notes _____
   Other (_____) _____
   Other (_____) _____

8. **Enter./Recreation** _____
   Eating Out _____
   Activities/Trips _____
   Vacation _____
   Other (_____) _____
   Other (_____) _____

9. **Clothing** _____

10. **Savings** _____

11. **Medical Expenses** _____
   Doctor _____
   Dentist _____
   Drugs _____
   Other _____

12. **Miscellaneous** _____
   Toiletry, cosmetics _____
   Beauty, barber _____
   Laundry, cleaning _____
   Allowances, lunches _____
   Subscriptions _____
   Gifts (incl. Christmas) _____
   Cash _____
   Other (_____) _____
   Other (_____) _____

13. **Investments** _____

14. **School/Child Care** _____
   Tuition _____
   Materials _____
   Transportion _____
   Day Care _____
   Other (_____) _____

   TOTAL EXPENSES _____

INCOME VERSUS EXPENSES
   Net Spendable Income _____
   Less Expenses _____

15. **Unallocated Surplus Income**[1] _____

---

1. This category is used when surplus income is received. This would be kept in the checking account to be used within a few weeks; otherwise, it should be transferred to an allocated category.

FORM 1

MONTHLY INCOME AND EXPENSES

GROSS INCOME PER MONTH _____

    Salary _____
    Interest _____
    Dividends _____
    Other (_____) _____
    Other (_____) _____

LESS:

1. **Tithe** _____

2. **Tax** (Est.-Incl. Fed., State, FICA) _____

    NET SPENDABLE INCOME _____

3. **Housing** _____
    Mortgage (rent) _____
    Insurance _____
    Taxes _____
    Electricity _____
    Gas _____
    Water _____
    Sanitation _____
    Telephone _____
    Maintenance _____
    Other (_____) _____
    Other (_____) _____

4. **Food** _____

5. **Automobile(s)** _____
    Payments _____
    Gas and Oil _____
    Insurance _____
    License / Taxes _____
    Maint. / Repair / Replace _____

6. **Insurance** _____
    Life _____
    Medical _____
    Other (_____) _____

7. **Debts** _____
    Credit Card _____
    Loans and Notes _____
    Other (_____) _____
    Other (_____) _____

8. **Enter./Recreation** _____
    Eating Out _____
    Activities / Trips _____
    Vacation _____
    Other (_____) _____
    Other (_____) _____

9. **Clothing** _____

10. **Savings** _____

11. **Medical Expenses** _____
    Doctor _____
    Dentist _____
    Drugs _____
    Other _____

12. **Miscellaneous** _____
    Toiletry, cosmetics _____
    Beauty, barber _____
    Laundry, cleaning _____
    Allowances, lunches _____
    Subscriptions _____
    Gifts (incl. Christmas) _____
    Cash _____
    Other (_____) _____
    Other (_____) _____

13. **Investments** _____

14. **School/Child Care** _____
    Tuition _____
    Materials _____
    Transportion _____
    Day Care _____
    Other (_____) _____

    TOTAL EXPENSES _____

INCOME VERSUS EXPENSES
    Net Spendable Income _____
    Less Expenses _____
    _____

15. **Unallocated Surplus Income**[1] _____

---

1. This category is used when surplus income is received. This would be kept in the checking account to be used within a few weeks; otherwise, it should be transferred to an allocated category.

FORM 1

MONTHLY INCOME AND EXPENSES

GROSS INCOME PER MONTH _____

    Salary _____

    Interest _____

    Dividends _____

    Other (_____) _____

    Other (_____) _____

LESS:

1. **Tithe** _____

2. **Tax** (Est.-Incl. Fed., State, FICA) _____

    NET SPENDABLE INCOME _____

3. **Housing** _____

    Mortgage (rent) _____

    Insurance _____

    Taxes _____

    Electricity _____

    Gas _____

    Water _____

    Sanitation _____

    Telephone _____

    Maintenance _____

    Other (_____) _____

    Other (_____) _____

4. **Food** _____

5. **Automobile(s)** _____

    Payments _____

    Gas and Oil _____

    Insurance _____

    License/Taxes _____

    Maint./Repair/Replace _____

6. **Insurance** _____

    Life _____

    Medical _____

    Other (_____) _____

7. **Debts** _____

    Credit Card _____

    Loans and Notes _____

    Other (_____) _____

    Other (_____) _____

8. **Enter./Recreation** _____

    Eating Out _____

    Activities/Trips _____

    Vacation _____

    Other (_____) _____

    Other (_____) _____

9. **Clothing** _____

10. **Savings** _____

11. **Medical Expenses** _____

    Doctor _____

    Dentist _____

    Drugs _____

    Other _____

12. **Miscellaneous** _____

    Toiletry, cosmetics _____

    Beauty, barber _____

    Laundry, cleaning _____

    Allowances, lunches _____

    Subscriptions _____

    Gifts (incl. Christmas) _____

    Cash _____

    Other (_____) _____

    Other (_____) _____

13. **Investments** _____

14. **School/Child Care** _____

    Tuition _____

    Materials _____

    Transportion _____

    Day Care _____

    Other (_____) _____

    TOTAL EXPENSES _____

INCOME VERSUS EXPENSES

    Net Spendable Income _____

    Less Expenses _____

15. **Unallocated Surplus Income**[1] _____

1. This category is used when surplus income is received. This would be kept in the checking account to be used within a few weeks; otherwise, it should be transferred to an allocated category.

FORM 1

MONTHLY INCOME AND EXPENSES

GROSS INCOME PER MONTH _____
- Salary _____
- Interest _____
- Dividends _____
- Other (_____) _____
- Other (_____) _____

LESS:

1. Tithe _____

2. Tax (Est.-Incl. Fed., State, FICA) _____

NET SPENDABLE INCOME _____

3. Housing _____
- Mortgage (rent) _____
- Insurance _____
- Taxes _____
- Electricity _____
- Gas _____
- Water _____
- Sanitation _____
- Telephone _____
- Maintenance _____
- Other (_____) _____
- Other (_____) _____

4. Food _____

5. Automobile(s) _____
- Payments _____
- Gas and Oil _____
- Insurance _____
- License/Taxes _____
- Maint./Repair/Replace _____

6. Insurance _____
- Life _____
- Medical _____
- Other (_____) _____

7. Debts _____
- Credit Card _____
- Loans and Notes _____
- Other (_____) _____
- Other (_____) _____

8. Enter./Recreation _____
- Eating Out _____
- Activities/Trips _____
- Vacation _____
- Other (_____) _____
- Other (_____) _____

9. Clothing _____

10. Savings _____

11. Medical Expenses _____
- Doctor _____
- Dentist _____
- Drugs _____
- Other _____

12. Miscellaneous _____
- Toiletry, cosmetics _____
- Beauty, barber _____
- Laundry, cleaning _____
- Allowances, lunches _____
- Subscriptions _____
- Gifts (incl. Christmas) _____
- Cash _____
- Other (_____) _____
- Other (_____) _____

13. Investments _____

14. School/Child Care _____
- Tuition _____
- Materials _____
- Transportion _____
- Day Care _____
- Other (_____) _____

TOTAL EXPENSES _____

INCOME VERSUS EXPENSES
- **Net Spendable Income** _____
- **Less Expenses** _____
_____

15. Unallocated Surplus Income[1] _____

1. This category is used when surplus income is received. This would be kept in the checking account to be used within a few weeks; otherwise, it should be transferred to an allocated category.

FORM 1

MONTHLY INCOME AND EXPENSES

GROSS INCOME PER MONTH _____

  Salary _____
  Interest _____
  Dividends _____
  Other (_____) _____
  Other (_____) _____

LESS:

1. Tithe _____

2. Tax (Est.-Incl. Fed., State, FICA) _____

  NET SPENDABLE INCOME _____

3. Housing _____
  Mortgage (rent) _____
  Insurance _____
  Taxes _____
  Electricity _____
  Gas _____
  Water _____
  Sanitation _____
  Telephone _____
  Maintenance _____
  Other (_____) _____
  Other (_____) _____

4. Food _____

5. Automobile(s) _____
  Payments _____
  Gas and Oil _____
  Insurance _____
  License/Taxes _____
  Maint./Repair/Replace _____

6. Insurance _____
  Life _____
  Medical _____
  Other (_____) _____

7. Debts _____
  Credit Card _____
  Loans and Notes _____
  Other (_____) _____
  Other (_____) _____

8. Enter./Recreation _____
  Eating Out _____
  Activities/Trips _____
  Vacation _____
  Other (_____) _____
  Other (_____) _____

9. Clothing _____

10. Savings _____

11. Medical Expenses _____
  Doctor _____
  Dentist _____
  Drugs _____
  Other _____

12. Miscellaneous _____
  Toiletry, cosmetics _____
  Beauty, barber _____
  Laundry, cleaning _____
  Allowances, lunches _____
  Subscriptions _____
  Gifts (incl. Christmas) _____
  Cash _____
  Other (_____) _____
  Other (_____) _____

13. Investments _____

14. School/Child Care _____
  Tuition _____
  Materials _____
  Transportion _____
  Day Care _____
  Other (_____) _____

  TOTAL EXPENSES _____

INCOME VERSUS EXPENSES
  Net Spendable Income _____
  Less Expenses _____

15. Unallocated Surplus Income[1] _____

---

1. This category is used when surplus income is received. This would be kept in the checking account to be used within a few weeks; otherwise, it should be transferred to an allocated category.

FORM 1

MONTHLY INCOME AND EXPENSES

GROSS INCOME PER MONTH _____

    Salary _____
    Interest _____
    Dividends _____
    Other (_____) _____
    Other (_____) _____

LESS:

  1. **Tithe** _____

  2. **Tax** (Est.-Incl. Fed., State, FICA) _____

    NET SPENDABLE INCOME _____

  3. **Housing** _____
    Mortgage (rent) _____
    Insurance _____
    Taxes _____
    Electricity _____
    Gas _____
    Water _____
    Sanitation _____
    Telephone _____
    Maintenance _____
    Other (_____) _____
    Other (_____) _____

  4. **Food** _____

  5. **Automobile(s)** _____
    Payments _____
    Gas and Oil _____
    Insurance _____
    License/Taxes _____
    Maint./Repair/Replace _____

  6. **Insurance** _____
    Life _____
    Medical _____
    Other (_____) _____

  7. **Debts** _____
    Credit Card _____
    Loans and Notes _____
    Other (_____) _____
    Other (_____) _____

  8. **Enter./Recreation** _____
    Eating Out _____
    Activities/Trips _____
    Vacation _____
    Other (_____) _____
    Other (_____) _____

  9. **Clothing** _____

  10. **Savings** _____

  11. **Medical Expenses** _____
    Doctor _____
    Dentist _____
    Drugs _____
    Other _____

  12. **Miscellaneous** _____
    Toiletry, cosmetics _____
    Beauty, barber _____
    Laundry, cleaning _____
    Allowances, lunches _____
    Subscriptions _____
    Gifts (incl. Christmas) _____
    Cash _____
    Other (_____) _____
    Other (_____) _____

  13. **Investments** _____

  14. **School/Child Care** _____
    Tuition _____
    Materials _____
    Transportion _____
    Day Care _____
    Other (_____) _____

    TOTAL EXPENSES _____

INCOME VERSUS EXPENSES
    Net Spendable Income _____
    Less Expenses _____

  15. **Unallocated Surplus Income**[1] _____

1. This category is used when surplus income is received. This would be kept in the checking account to be used within a few weeks; otherwise, it should be transferred to an allocated category.

FORM 1

VARIABLE EXPENSE PLANNING

Plan for expenses that are not paid on a regular monthly basis by estimating the yearly cost and determining the monthly amount needed to be set aside for that expense. A helpful formula is to allow the previous year's expense plus 5 percent.

	Estimated Cost		Per Month
1. Vacation	$ _____	÷ 12 =	$ _____
2. Dentist	$ _____	÷ 12 =	$ _____
3. Doctor	$ _____	÷ 12 =	$ _____
4. Auto	$ _____	÷ 12 =	$ _____
5. Annual Insurance	$ _____	÷ 12 =	$ _____
(Life)	($ _____	÷ 12 =	$ _____)
(Health)	($ _____	÷ 12 =	$ _____)
(Auto)	($ _____	÷ 12 =	$ _____)
(Home)	($ _____	÷ 12 =	$ _____)
6. Clothing	$ _____	÷ 12 =	$ _____
7. Investments	$ _____	÷ 12 =	$ _____
8. Other	$ _____	÷ 12 =	$ _____
	$ _____	÷ 12 =	$ _____

FORM 2

VARIABLE EXPENSE PLANNING

Plan for expenses that are not paid on a regular monthly basis by estimating the yearly cost and determining the monthly amount needed to be set aside for that expense. A helpful formula is to allow the previous year's expense plus 5 percent.

	Estimated Cost		Per Month
1. Vacation	$ _____	÷ 12 =	$ _____
2. Dentist	$ _____	÷ 12 =	$ _____
3. Doctor	$ _____	÷ 12 =	$ _____
4. Auto	$ _____	÷ 12 =	$ _____
5. Annual Insurance	$ _____	÷ 12 =	$ _____
(Life)	($ _____	÷ 12 =	$ _____)
(Health)	($ _____	÷ 12 =	$ _____)
(Auto)	($ _____	÷ 12 =	$ _____)
(Home)	($ _____	÷ 12 =	$ _____)
6. Clothing	$ _____	÷ 12 =	$ _____
7. Investments	$ _____	÷ 12 =	$ _____
8. Other	$ _____	÷ 12 =	$ _____
	$ _____	÷ 12 =	$ _____

FORM 2

VARIABLE EXPENSE PLANNING

Plan for expenses that are not paid on a regular monthly basis by estimating the yearly cost and determining the monthly amount needed to be set aside for that expense. A helpful formula is to allow the previous year's expense plus 5 percent.

	Estimated Cost		Per Month
1. Vacation	$ _____	÷ 12 =	$ _____
2. Dentist	$ _____	÷ 12 =	$ _____
3. Doctor	$ _____	÷ 12 =	$ _____
4. Auto	$ _____	÷ 12 =	$ _____
5. Annual Insurance	$ _____	÷ 12 =	$ _____
(Life)	($ _____	÷ 12 =	$ _____)
(Health)	($ _____	÷ 12 =	$ _____)
(Auto)	($ _____	÷ 12 =	$ _____)
(Home)	($ _____	÷ 12 =	$ _____)
6. Clothing	$ _____	÷ 12 =	$ _____
7. Investments	$ _____	÷ 12 =	$ _____
8. Other	$ _____	÷ 12 =	$ _____
	$ _____	÷ 12 =	$ _____

FORM 2

VARIABLE EXPENSE PLANNING

Plan for expenses that are not paid on a regular monthly basis by estimating the yearly cost and determining the monthly amount needed to be set aside for that expense. A helpful formula is to allow the previous year's expense plus 5 percent.

	Estimated Cost	Per Month
1. Vacation	$ _____ ÷ 12 =	$ _____
2. Dentist	$ _____ ÷ 12 =	$ _____
3. Doctor	$ _____ ÷ 12 =	$ _____
4. Auto	$ _____ ÷ 12 =	$ _____
5. Annual Insurance	$ _____ ÷ 12 =	$ _____
(Life)	($ _____ ÷ 12 =	$ _____)
(Health)	($ _____ ÷ 12 =	$ _____)
(Auto)	($ _____ ÷ 12 =	$ _____)
(Home)	($ _____ ÷ 12 =	$ _____)
6. Clothing	$ _____ ÷ 12 =	$ _____
7. Investments	$ _____ ÷ 12 =	$ _____
8. Other	$ _____ ÷ 12 =	$ _____
	$ _____ ÷ 12 =	$ _____

FORM 2

BUDGET PERCENTAGE GUIDELINES

Salary for guideline = $_____/year

Gross Income Per Month $_____

1. **Tithe**   (___% of Gross) (_____) = $ _____

2. **Tax**   (___% of Gross) (_____) = $ _____

Net Spendable Income $_____

3. **Housing**   (___% of Net)   (_____) = $ _____

4. **Food**   (___% of Net)   (_____) = $ _____

5. **Auto**   (___% of Net)   (_____) = $ _____

6. **Insurance**   (___% of Net)   (_____) = $ _____

7. **Debts**   (___% of Net)   (_____) = $ _____

8. **Entertainment/ Recreation** (___% of Net)   (_____) = $ _____

9. **Clothing**   (___% of Net)   (_____) = $ _____

10. **Savings**   (___% of Net)   (_____) = $ _____

11. **Medical**   (___% of Net)   (_____) = $ _____

12. **Miscellaneous**   (___% of Net)   (_____) = $ _____

13. **Investments**   (___% of Net)   (_____) = $ _____

14. **School/ Child Care** (___% of Net)   (_____) = $ _____

Total (Cannot exceed Net Spendable Income) $ _____

15. **Unallocated Surplus Income**   (___N/A___) = $ _____

FORM 3

BUDGET PERCENTAGE GUIDELINES

Salary for guideline = $_____/year

Gross Income Per Month $_____

1. Tithe   (___% of Gross) (_____) = $ _____

2. Tax   (___% of Gross) (_____) = $ _____

Net Spendable Income $_____

3. Housing   (___% of Net)   (_____) = $ _____

4. Food   (___% of Net)   (_____) = $ _____

5. Auto   (___% of Net)   (_____) = $ _____

6. Insurance   (___% of Net)   (_____) = $ _____

7. Debts   (___% of Net)   (_____) = $ _____

8. Entertainment/   (___% of Net)   (_____) = $ _____
   Recreation

9. Clothing   (___% of Net)   (_____) = $ _____

10. Savings   (___% of Net)   (_____) = $ _____

11. Medical   (___% of Net)   (_____) = $ _____

12. Miscellaneous   (___% of Net)   (_____) = $ _____

13. Investments   (___% of Net)   (_____) = $ _____

14. School/   (___% of Net)   (_____) = $ _____
    Child Care

Total (Cannot exceed Net Spendable Income) $ _____

15. Unallocated Surplus Income   (____N/A____) = $ _____

FORM 3

BUDGET PERCENTAGE GUIDELINES

Salary for guideline = $_____/year

Gross Income Per Month $_____

  1. **Tithe**   (___% of Gross) (_____) = $ _____

  2. **Tax**   (___% of Gross) (_____) = $ _____

Net Spendable Income $_____

  3. **Housing**   (___% of Net) (_____) = $ _____

  4. **Food**   (___% of Net) (_____) = $ _____

  5. **Auto**   (___% of Net) (_____) = $ _____

  6. **Insurance**   (___% of Net) (_____) = $ _____

  7. **Debts**   (___% of Net) (_____) = $ _____

  8. **Entertainment/ Recreation** (___% of Net) (_____) = $ _____

  9. **Clothing**   (___% of Net) (_____) = $ _____

10. **Savings**   (___% of Net) (_____) = $ _____

11. **Medical**   (___% of Net) (_____) = $ _____

12. **Miscellaneous** (___% of Net) (_____) = $ _____

13. **Investments** (___% of Net) (_____) = $ _____

14. **School/ Child Care** (___% of Net) (_____) = $ _____

Total (Cannot exceed Net Spendable Income) $ _____

15. **Unallocated Surplus Income** (_____N/A_____) = $ _____

FORM 3

BUDGET PERCENTAGE GUIDELINES

Salary for guideline = $_____/year

Gross Income Per Month $_____

  1. Tithe   (___% of Gross) (_____) = $ _____

  2. Tax   (___% of Gross) (_____) = $ _____

Net Spendable Income $_____

  3. Housing   (___% of Net) (_____) = $ _____

  4. Food   (___% of Net) (_____) = $ _____

  5. Auto   (___% of Net) (_____) = $ _____

  6. Insurance   (___% of Net) (_____) = $ _____

  7. Debts   (___% of Net) (_____) = $ _____

  8. Entertainment/ (___% of Net) (_____) = $ _____
     Recreation

  9. Clothing   (___% of Net) (_____) = $ _____

10. Savings   (___% of Net) (_____) = $ _____

11. Medical   (___% of Net) (_____) = $ _____

12. Miscellaneous (___% of Net) (_____) = $ _____

13. Investments   (___% of Net) (_____) = $ _____

14. School/   (___% of Net) (_____) = $ _____
     Child Care

Total (Cannot exceed Net Spendable Income) $ _____

15. Unallocated Surplus Income   (_____N/A_____) = $ _____

FORM 3

108

BUDGET ANALYSIS

Per Year $_____   Net Spendable Income
Per Month $_____   Per Month $_____

MONTHLY PAYMENT CATEGORY	EXISTING BUDGET	MONTHLY GUIDELINE BUDGET	DIFFERENCE + OR -	NEW MONTHLY BUDGET
1. Tithe				
2. Tax				
Net Spendable Income (per month)	$_____	$_____	$_____	$_____
3. Housing				
4. Food				
5. Auto				
6. Insurance				
7. Debts				
8. Enter./Recreation				
9. Clothing				
10. Savings				
11. Medical				
12. Miscellaneous				
13. Investments				
14. School/Child Care				
Totals (Items 3-14)	$_____	$_____		$_____
15. Unallocated Surplus Income				

FORM 4

BUDGET ANALYSIS

Per Year $_____

Per Month $_____

Net Spendable Income
Per Month $_____

MONTHLY PAYMENT CATEGORY	EXISTING BUDGET	MONTHLY GUIDELINE BUDGET	DIFFERENCE + OR -	NEW MONTHLY BUDGET
1. Tithe				
2. Tax				
Net Spendable Income (per month)	$_____	$_____	$_____	$_____
3. Housing				
4. Food				
5. Auto				
6. Insurance				
7. Debts				
8. Enter./Recreation				
9. Clothing				
10. Savings				
11. Medical				
12. Miscellaneous				
13. Investments				
14. School/Child Care				
Totals (Items 3-14)	$_____	$_____		$_____
15. Unallocated Surplus Income				

FORM 4

BUDGET ANALYSIS

Per Year $_____

Per Month $_____

Net Spendable Income
Per Month $_____

MONTHLY PAYMENT CATEGORY	EXISTING BUDGET	MONTHLY GUIDELINE BUDGET	DIFFERENCE + OR -	NEW MONTHLY BUDGET
1. Tithe				
2. Tax				
Net Spendable Income (per month)	$_____	$_____	$_____	$_____
3. Housing				
4. Food				
5. Auto				
6. Insurance				
7. Debts				
8. Enter./Recreation				
9. Clothing				
10. Savings				
11. Medical				
12. Miscellaneous				
13. Investments				
14. School/Child Care				
Totals (Items 3-14)	$_____	$_____		$_____
15. Unallocated Surplus Income				

FORM 4

BUDGET ANALYSIS

Per Year $_____

Per Month $_____

Net Spendable Income
Per Month $_____

MONTHLY PAYMENT CATEGORY	EXISTING BUDGET	MONTHLY GUIDELINE BUDGET	DIFFERENCE + OR -	NEW MONTHLY BUDGET
1. Tithe				
2. Tax				
Net Spendable Income (per month)	$_____	$_____	$_____	$_____
3. Housing				
4. Food				
5. Auto				
6. Insurance				
7. Debts				
8. Enter./Recreation				
9. Clothing				
10. Savings				
11. Medical				
12. Miscellaneous				
13. Investments				
14. School/Child Care				
Totals (Items 3-14)	$_____	$_____		$_____

15. Unallocated Surplus Income				

FORM 4

INCOME ALLOCATION

INCOME		INCOME SOURCE/PAY PERIOD			
BUDGET CATEGORY	MONTHLY ALLOCATION				
1. Tithe					
2. Tax					
3. Housing					
4. Food					
5. Auto					
6. Insurance					
7. Debts					
8. Enter./Recreation					
9. Clothing					
10. Savings					
11. Medical					
12. Miscellaneous					
13. Investments					
14. School/Child Care					
15. Unallocated Surplus Income					

FORM 5

INCOME ALLOCATION

INCOME		INCOME SOURCE/PAY PERIOD			
BUDGET CATEGORY	MONTHLY ALLOCATION				
1. Tithe					
2. Tax					
3. Housing					
4. Food					
5. Auto					
6. Insurance					
7. Debts					
8. Enter./Recreation					
9. Clothing					
10. Savings					
11. Medical					
12. Miscellaneous					
13. Investments					
14. School/Child Care					
15. Unallocated Surplus Income					

FORM 5

INCOME ALLOCATION

INCOME		INCOME SOURCE/PAY PERIOD			
BUDGET CATEGORY	MONTHLY ALLOCATION				
1. Tithe					
2. Tax					
3. Housing					
4. Food					
5. Auto					
6. Insurance					
7. Debts					
8. Enter./Recreation					
9. Clothing					
10. Savings					
11. Medical					
12. Miscellaneous					
13. Investments					
14. School/Child Care					
15. Unallocated Surplus Income					

FORM 5

INCOME ALLOCATION

		INCOME SOURCE/PAY PERIOD			
INCOME					
BUDGET CATEGORY	**MONTHLY ALLOCATION**				
1. Tithe					
2. Tax					
3. Housing					
4. Food					
5. Auto					
6. Insurance					
7. Debts					
8. Enter./Recreation					
9. Clothing					
10. Savings					
11. Medical					
12. Miscellaneous					
13. Investments					
14. School/Child Care					
15. Unallocated Surplus Income					

FORM 5

SAVINGS ACCOUNT ALLOCATIONS

Date	Deposit	With-drawal	Balance	Housing	Food	Auto Insur.	Auto Maint.	Insur-ance	Clothing	Medical	Debts		

FORM 6

SAVINGS ACCOUNT ALLOCATIONS

Date	Deposit	With-drawal	Balance	Housing	Food	Auto Insur.	Auto Maint.	Insur-ance	Clothing	Medical	Debts					

FORM 6

SAVINGS ACCOUNT ALLOCATIONS

Date	Deposit	With-drawal	Balance	Housing	Food	Auto Insur.	Auto Maint.	Insur-ance	Clothing	Medical	Debts			

FORM 6

SAVINGS ACCOUNT ALLOCATIONS

Date	Deposit	With-drawal	Balance	Housing	Food	Auto Insur.	Auto Maint.	Insur-ance	Clothing	Medical	Debts				

FORM 6

INDIVIDUAL ACCOUNT PAGE

_____ $ _____ $ _____
ACCOUNT CATEGORY   ALLOCATION   ALLOCATION

DATE	TRANSACTION	DEPOSIT	WITHDRAWAL	BALANCE

FORM 7

INDIVIDUAL ACCOUNT PAGE

ACCOUNT CATEGORY	$ ALLOCATION	$ ALLOCATION

DATE	TRANSACTION	DEPOSIT		WITHDRAWAL		BALANCE	

FORM 7

INDIVIDUAL ACCOUNT PAGE

	ACCOUNT CATEGORY	$ ALLOCATION	$ ALLOCATION

DATE	TRANSACTION	DEPOSIT	WITHDRAWAL	BALANCE

FORM 7

INDIVIDUAL ACCOUNT PAGE

		$		$	
	ACCOUNT CATEGORY		ALLOCATION		ALLOCATION

DATE	TRANSACTION	DEPOSIT	WITHDRAWAL	BALANCE

FORM 7

INDIVIDUAL ACCOUNT PAGE

<table>
<tr><td colspan="3">ACCOUNT CATEGORY</td><td>$ ALLOCATION</td><td>$ ALLOCATION</td></tr>
</table>

DATE	TRANSACTION	DEPOSIT		WITHDRAWAL		BALANCE	

FORM 7

INDIVIDUAL ACCOUNT PAGE

ACCOUNT CATEGORY	$ ALLOCATION	$ ALLOCATION

DATE	TRANSACTION	DEPOSIT		WITHDRAWAL		BALANCE	

FORM 7

CHECKBOOK LEDGER

DATE	CK. #	TRANSACTION	DEPOSIT	WITHDRAWAL	BALANCE

FORM 7a

CHECKBOOK LEDGER

DATE	CK. #	TRANSACTION	DEPOSIT	WITHDRAWAL	BALANCE

FORM 7a

CHECKBOOK LEDGER

DATE	CK. #	TRANSACTION		DEPOSIT		WITHDRAWAL		BALANCE	

FORM 7a

CHECKBOOK LEDGER

DATE	CK. #	TRANSACTION	DEPOSIT	WITHDRAWAL	BALANCE

FORM 7a

LIST OF DEBTS

as of _____

TO WHOM OWED	CONTACT NAME PHONE NUMBER	PAY OFF	PAYMENTS LEFT	MONTHLY PAYMENT	DUE DATE

FORM 8

LIST OF DEBTS

as of _____

TO WHOM OWED	CONTACT NAME PHONE NUMBER	PAY OFF	PAYMENTS LEFT	MONTHLY PAYMENT	DUE DATE

FORM 8

IMPULSE LIST

DATE	IMPULSE ITEM	1	2	3

IMPULSE LIST

DATE	IMPULSE ITEM	1	2	3

FORM 9

IMPULSE LIST

DATE	IMPULSE ITEM	1	2	3

IMPULSE LIST

DATE	IMPULSE ITEM	1	2	3

FORM 9

IMPULSE LIST

DATE	IMPULSE ITEM	1	2	3

IMPULSE LIST

DATE	IMPULSE ITEM	1	2	3

FORM 9

IMPULSE LIST

DATE	IMPULSE ITEM	1	2	3

IMPULSE LIST

DATE	IMPULSE ITEM	1	2	3

FORM 9